Classroom Teaching Skills

A Primer

Kenneth D. Moore

Cameron University

Random House New York

This book was developed by Lane Akers, Inc.

First Edition

98765432

Copyright © 1989 by Random House, Inc.

Library of Congress Cataloging-in-Publication Data

Moore, Kenneth D.
    Classroom teaching skills : a primer / Kenneth D. Moore. — 1st
  ed.
        p.   cm.
    Includes index.
    ISBN 0-394-38151-3
    1. Teaching—Handbooks, manuals, etc.   2. Classroom management—
Handbooks, manuals, etc.   I. Title.
LB1025.2M569   1989
371.1'02—dc19   88-11607
                                                                      CIP

Photo credits: p. 2, Christopher Brown/Stock, Boston; p. 16, Wasyl Szkodzinsky/ Photo Researchers; p. 42, Sarah Putnam/The Picture Cube; p. 70, Susan Lapides/Design Conceptions; p. 90, Arthur Grace/Stock, Boston; p. 112, Susan McElhinney, Archive; p. 138, Jim Anderson/Woodfin Camp and Assoc.; p. 150, Ulrike Welsch/Photo Researchers; p. 168, Paul Fortin/Stock, Boston; p. 194, Richard Hutchings/Photo Researchers

Preface

Every profession has at its core a repertoire of essential skills that every dedicated practitioner attempts to master. Of course, no one completely masters any skill; one simply becomes more proficient as a result of ongoing study and practice. Those who are most dedicated and eventually become most proficient are generally the ones who are least satisfied with their own level of mastery. In short, true professionals are never satisfied; they are continually looking for tools that will help them sharpen their skills.

Classroom Teaching Skills: A Primer was written with the believe that both preservice and practicing teachers can benefit from a text that presents essential teaching skills in a concise, easy-to-read fashion. Organized around a comprehensive model of teaching that includes planning, implementation, and evaluation components, the skills addressed in this volume are common to instruction at all grade levels and in all subject areas. Taken together they might be thought of as a minimum repertoire of skills that all teachers need to acquire.

Because it is brief, affordable, and self-instructional, this book can be used as a core text for skills-oriented general methods courses; as a supplementary text for elementary and secondary methods courses; or as a handy reference tool for in-service seminars and workshops with a practical skills focus. It also makes an ideal reference volume for individuals wanting a skills refresher prior to taking state or national competency exams.

The text has been carefully designed in order to maximize its instructional flexibility and to model established principles of instruction. Each chapter begins with specific learning objectives that help focus the reader's attention. The reader's understanding of key concepts is then checked through a series of self-tests that appear at the end of subsections within the chapters. End-of-chapter answer keys provide immediate feedback on how well the chapter objectives were met.

Preservice students will find more here than can possibly be absorbed in a single course, even one that is liberally supported by episodes of practice teaching. They should view this book as a flexible tool that should initially be read and studied and then periodically revisited, much as English students reference their handbooks of grammar and usage. Since the skills presented here apply to almost all teacher education courses, this volume might be thought of as a "text for all seasons."

Practicing teachers will find this highly organized, densely packed little volume the most compact skills reference tool available. Since these skills now appear on most state and national lists of basic teaching competencies, its value can hardly be overestimated. A handy guide that accompanies the book keys its contents to the professional knowledge section of major state and national teacher exams.

A textbook represents the cooperative efforts and experiences of many individuals who help in shaping its form and content. In this respect, I would like to express my gratitude and appreciation to all of the teachers and students whose contributions appear throughout the book. Thanks go to Patricia Hanley at the University of South Florida and Marsha Grace at the University of Houston, Victoria, for their critical review of the manuscript. I would especially like to thank Lane Akers for his criticism, editing, and guidance in the production of this book. I would like to express my appreciation to Eileen Thomas, the secretary who made the writing-typing process an interesting exchange of ideas and opinions. And finally, I thank Jean Akers for her professionalism, aid in editing, and preparation of the manuscript for publication. My final words are encouragement for my son, Nicholas Dean, who will persevere despite the tribulations that he must endure in life.

K.D.M.

Contents

Chapter 10   Classroom Management   195

part 1

THE TOOLS OF TEACHING

Teaching is a challenge that requires long hours of work and preparation. But above all it requires skill in planning and skill in the classroom.

The purpose of this first section is to help you gain insight into the process of teaching and to put that process into a framework that will assist you in preparing to teach. Chapter 1 addresses what it means to teach. We discuss the different roles of a teacher and develop a working definition of teaching. Also, since planning forms the core of the teaching process, a comprehensive seven-step planning model is presented. Various preinstructional, instructional, and postinstructional teaching skills associated with this model are then identified and described.

Observations often provide needed data for the ongoing planning process as well as for managing the interactive dynamics of the classroom. Hence, Chapter 2 provides a framework for making accurate observations to be used both in planning and during the instructional process.

The Teaching Process

After completing your study of Chapter 1, you should be able to:

1. Identify and describe the three major roles performed by teachers
2. Define teaching
3. Identify the teaching skills necessary for effective teaching at the elementary and secondary level
4. Explain the importance of effective planning
5. Identify and describe the seven sequential steps to the planning process
6. Explain the cyclic nature of the planning process
7. Identify and describe various generic teaching skills

One of the proudest and most important moments in the life of a teacher is the teaching of that first class. If you are an experienced teacher, that first day has come and gone and is recalled with fond memories. Or is it? If you are a novice teacher, you are probably looking forward to that first day with great anticipation. The hours of work and preparation will finally pay off!

Whether you are an experienced teacher or a novice, you probably have some misgivings and apprehension about the teaching profession. Most likely you have concerns about being a "successful" teacher, a "good" teacher, an "effective" teacher.

What makes an effective teacher? Are there certain identifiable skills that make one teacher more effective than another? Some will say that effective teachers are born with the skill to teach. Others scoff at this notion and declare that it is possible to develop and train someone to be an effective teacher. This text identifies with the latter group.

TEACHING

What does it mean to teach? We must answer this question before we can decide whether someone is an effective teacher. To prepare for developing a formal definition of teaching, let us look at what a teacher does. What are the major roles of a teacher?

Roles of a Teacher

Teachers play many roles, some of which interlock and overlap. However, most of your teaching activities can be divided into three broad categories that describe what you as a teacher do to bring about desired learning and changes in student behavior and to enhance student development.

Instructional Expert   The first and most notable role performed by a teacher is that of instructional expert: the person who plans, guides, and evaluates learning. This role, in a sense, serves as a kind of core role that the others tend to support.

As an instructional expert, you must make decisions related to what to teach, what teaching materials to use, the best method to teach the selected content, and how to evaluate the intended learning. These decisions will be based on a number of factors, including state-suggested curricular goals, your knowledge of the subject, your knowledge of learning theory and motivation, the abilities and needs of your students, your own personality and needs, and your overall teaching goals.

Students will expect you, as an instructional expert, to have all the answers, not only to questions about your subject but to a multitude of subjects.

Manager The second important job that a teacher has is to order and to structure the learning environment. Included in this role are all the decisions and actions required to maintain order in the classroom, such as laying down rules and procedures for learning activities. Sometimes this role is viewed as nothing more than that of disciplinarian, the person who must see that the classroom group and its individual members stay within the limits set by the school, the limits set by you the teacher, and the limits set by the tasks at hand. However, in its best sense, management is much more complex.

Teachers must manage a classroom environment. Therefore, teachers are environmental engineers who organize the classroom space to fit their goals and to maximize learning. The way the physical space of the classroom is organized can either help or hinder learning. Seating must be arranged; posters hung; bulletin boards decorated; extra books, learning carrels, and bookshelves installed. You may even want to build or adapt furniture for use in your classroom.

Classroom management also involves modeling a positive attitude toward the curriculum and toward school and learning in general. Teachers who reveal a caring attitude toward learning and the learning environment help instill and reinforce similar attitudes in their students. The results, hopefully, will be more self-disciplined students and fewer management problems.

Finally, teachers are required to manage and process great amounts of clerical work. There are papers to be read and graded, tests to be scored, marks to be entered, attendance records and files to be maintained, notes and letters to be written, and so forth. Sometimes there seems to be little time for anything else.

Counselor Although you will not be a trained counselor or psychologist, you should be a sensitive observer of human behavior. You must be prepared to respond constructively when behavior problems get in the way of student learning and development. In almost every class there are students who will look to you for guidance. Thus you must be prepared to assist students and parents with these problems and be prepared to work with colleagues in making the school experience as supportive as possible.

Remember that teachers work with people: students, parents, administrators, and colleagues. You must possess good human relations skills and be prepared to communicate and work with these different factions on a day-to-day basis, sometimes under unpleasant circumstances. These interactions, both pleasant and unpleasant, will benefit from a deep understanding of people and their behaviors. Finally, you will need a thorough understanding of yourself—your own motivations, hopes, prejudices, and desires —all of which will effect your ability to relate to others.

Do you feel overwhelmed by all these aspects of teaching? You may be surprised to learn that many experienced teachers are too. With these roles in mind, let us develop a formal definition of teaching.

A Definition of Teaching

There are many definitions for the term **teaching**. *The Random House College Dictionary* defines teaching as the action of a person "to impart knowledge or skill to; give instruction to"; or "the act or profession of a person who teaches." Clark and Starr (1986) suggest teaching is an attempt to assist students in acquiring or changing some skill, knowledge, ideal, attitude, or appreciation. Bruner (1966) defines instruction as "an effort to assist or shape growth" (p. 1). These definitions and the roles that teachers perform imply that teachers need to be concerned with all aspects of student development—physical, social, emotional, and cognitive. Therefore, a broad definition of teaching might be: the actions of someone who is trying to assist others to reach their fullest potential in all aspects of development. This is a tall order. What skills might one need in order to accomplish this noble task?

SPECIFIC TEACHING SKILLS

Joyce and Weil (1980) suggest there are many kinds of effective teachers. They further suggest that different teachers are effective under different circumstances. For example, a teacher might be quite effective at the elementary level but quite ineffective at the secondary level, or vice versa. Since elementary teachers are required to teach all areas of the curriculum, whereas secondary teachers usually teach in only one or two curriculum areas, subject matter instruction will usually be much deeper at the secondary level. Thus, when observing instruction at the elementary and secondary levels, you should note which specific skills are necessary for effective teaching at each level.

Skill in teaching reading represents another area in which elementary and secondary teachers differ. Because elementary teachers are responsible for teaching basic reading skills, they need extensive training in teaching those skills. Although reading instruction has historically been neglected at the secondary level, the importance of refining secondary students' reading skills is now becoming apparent (Clark and Starr, 1986). In fact, many secondary teachers are now required to develop some skill in teaching content reading. Unfortunately, in most states skill in teaching reading is still required only of elementary teachers.

Major developmental differences between elementary and secondary level students also help differentiate the skills needed by teachers at different grade levels. At the secondary level, adolescents are going through puberty. They experience a spurt in growth patterns and are maturing sexually. These physical changes can lead to an exaggerated concern about appearance and size. Socially, adolescents try to achieve independence from the family and often become greatly influenced by peer groups and overly involved in extracurricular activities. Emotionally, there is a search for identity that can result in moodiness, experimentation with drugs and alcohol, and even suicide in extreme cases. At this stage, thinking becomes more complex, a value system is further developed and refined, and competencies for life goals are mastered. With all these changes, no wonder adjustment is a problem. Thus adolescent students need teachers who can model and help them acquire complex physical, social, emotional, and cognitive skills. What is needed is a combination subject matter expert, counselor, social psychologist, mental health worker, and youth group worker.

In contrast students at the elementary level, particularly in the primary grades, are still quite dependent and need teachers who can display and provide affection and act as surrogate parents. As a result of these developmental differences, vastly different skills are needed to work effectively with elementary and secondary level students.

GENERIC TEACHING SKILLS

There are also certain teacher skills that are essential for effective teaching in all grades and in all curriculum areas. These generic skills can be classified as preinstructional, instructional, or postinstructional.

Preinstructional Skills

The key to effective teaching is planning (Jacobsen et al., 1985). You must plan well to teach well. But what skills does one need in order to plan well? To answer this question, let us take a closer look at the planning process. Essentially, **planning** can be thought of as a sequential decision-making process. You must decide sequentially on answers to the following:

1. What content should be taught?

2. What are the desired learner outcomes?

3. What teaching materials will be needed?

4. What is the best way to introduce the subject?

5. What is the best instructional strategy for the intended learning?

6. How should the lesson be closed?

7. How should the students be evaluated?

This sequential planning process is illustrated in Figure 1.1. Step 1 involves identifying the content; Step 2, writing objectives; Step 3, introducing the lesson; Step 4, selecting an instructional strategy; Step 5, closing the lesson; Step 6, evaluating the lesson; and Step 7, identifying new content to be taught. Notice that Step 7 uses the evaluative information of Step 6 to determine the next

FIGURE 1.1 Basic Seven-Step Planning Process.   The process is both sequential and cyclic in nature. Steps 3, 4, and 5 represent the component of the process that is implemented in the classroom.

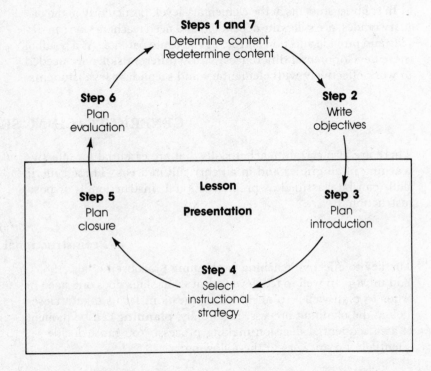

lesson's content. Also, note that Steps 3, 4, and 5 involve activities that form the class presentation component of the model. We will take a brief look at each of these steps before discussing them at length in subsequent chapters.

Step 1 involves selecting the content to be taught. The content can be determined by analyzing state-mandated learner outcomes and curriculum guides, by examining recommended textbooks, or by analyzing (diagnosing) student needs. Student needs are usually determined from past class evaluations (Step 6) and from class observations during past lessons.

Once the content has been selected, Step 2 is to decide exactly what students should know and exactly what attitudes and values should be developed with regard to that content. These specifics are stated in your lesson objectives and should be expressed in performance terms. In other words, objectives should specify exactly what students should be able to do upon completion of the lesson or the unit of study.

In Step 3, the lesson introduction, your objective is to gain the undivided attention of the students. This introduction is commonly referred to as the **set induction** or the establishment of a **cognitive set**.

The selection of an instructional strategy is Step 4 in the planning model and is of prime importance. Your task is to select the strategy that best fits your students' maturity levels, learning styles, and the classroom environment. This selection is determined from your knowledge of learning theory and from past observations of the class.

Step 5 involves ending the lesson. The closing must be planned so that the lesson content is made meaningful and is fully understood. This is referred to as your **lesson closure**.

Finally, (Step 6) you must determine whether you have accomplished what you wanted. You must determine whether the students have mastered the specifics you have written into your objectives. However, your evaluation is not the end of the process; it is merely the starting point for the next planning cycle.

As you can see, the planning process represents a major undertaking that is essential to effective teaching. You can now check your understanding of the planning process by completing Tasks 1.1 and 1.2.

A thorough examination of the preinstructional and planning process reveals that it is a major undertaking requiring a number of skills. Specifically, you must be able to:

1. Make accurate observations

2. Write objectives

3. Select instructional materials

4. Plan appropriate cognitive sets (set inductions)

5. Select appropriate teaching strategies

6. Plan appropriate closures

7. Determine and develop appropriate evaluations

Whether you are a future teacher or an experienced one, you need to develop and refine these preinstructional skills. The results will be more effective planning and increased student learning.

TASK 1.1 Listing the Planning Steps

List the seven steps to the planning process in sequential order. Check your responses with those given at the end of the chapter.

Step 1: _____

Step 2: _____

Step 3: _____

Step 4: _____

Step 5: _____

Step 6: _____

Step 7: _____

TASK 1.2 Identifying the Planning Steps

The following items should be addressed in the planning process. Indicate which step of the seven-step planning process addresses each item. Check your responses with those given at the end of the chapter.

_____ 1. An activity is planned to capture the undivided attention of the students.

_____ 2. The specifics that students should learn are identified.

_____ 3. The level of learning by the students is checked.

_____ 4. The activities to be used in teaching the content are developed or selected.

_____ 5. The content to be taught is determined.

Instructional Skills

Once you have planned a lesson, you must implement it. Implementing a lesson so that maximum learning takes place is a difficult task that requires special skills essential to all teachers.

Central to instruction is the ability to communicate. You cannot teach effectively if you are unable to communicate with your students. Moreover, you cannot communicate effectively without gaining student attention and arousing and maintaining their interest. This requires skill in the use of stimulus variation, questions, and reinforcement.

Management of the learning environment is also a skill that all effective teachers must master (Charles, 1985). You must be able to get students' cooperation, maintain their involvement in learning tasks, and conduct the business of the classroom smoothly and efficiently. Little teaching or learning can take place in an environment that is not well managed. Without the skill to manage a classroom, even well-planned lessons can fail.

Successful implementation of a well-planned lesson requires a number of special skills. Specifically you must be able to:

1. Establish cognitive sets (set inductions)

2. Communicate

3. Use stimulus variation

4. Use reinforcement effectively

5. Use questioning techniques

6. Manage a classroom

7. Establish lesson closure

8. Evaluate objectives

Although the development and refinement of these instructional skills does not guarantee success, they should greatly increase your potential for success.

Postinstructional Skills

Teaching involves well-planned and organized evaluation. Evaluative information must be collected and analyzed with respect to your objectives, and judgments must be made regarding the level of student achievement. Consequently, data collection techniques, instrumentation, and data analysis techniques must be planned and developed prior to instruction.

There are two postinstructional skills essential to effective evaluation. Specifically, you must be able to analyze collected evaluative information and make judgments regarding evaluative information. Although these skills are used following instruction, they must be carefully planned prior to instruction.

The remainder of this book was written expressly to assist you in developing and refining your understanding and use of preinstructional and instructional teaching skills. Before going further, however, check your understanding of the material presented so far by completing Task 1.3.

TASK 1.3 Identifying Teaching Skills

Classify each skill or knowledge area as being needed only by elementary teachers (E), needed only by secondary teachers (S), or a general teaching skill or knowledge area needed by all teachers (G). Check your responses with those given at the end of the chapter.

_____ 1. Knowledge of the learning process

_____ 2. Skill in handling discipline problems

_____ 3. Skill in making observations

_____ 4. Refined skill in teaching basic reading

_____ 5. Skill in listening

_____ 6. Depth of knowledge in a single content area

_____ 7. Skill in writing objectives

_____ 8. Knowledge of adolescent behavior

_____ 9. Skill in lesson closing techniques

_____ 10. Skill in nonverbal communications

SUMMARY

Teachers are expected to be instructional experts, classroom managers, and to some extent educational psychologists. Many skills must be mastered to carry out these roles effectively.

Teaching skills fall into three distinct categories: preinstructional, instructional, and postinstructional. Preinstructional skills are those needed by teachers to be effective planners. They include the ability to (1) make observations, (2) write objectives, (3) select materials, (4) plan cognitive sets, (5) select teaching strategies, (6) plan closures, and (7) develop evaluations. Instructional skills consist of those skills needed by teachers to successfully implement planned lessons. These skills include the ability to (1) establish cognitive sets, (2) communicate, (3) provide stimulus variation, (4) use reinforcement, (5) use questions, (6) manage a classroom, (7) establish lesson closures, and (8) evaluate lesson objectives. Postinstructional skills are those skills needed by teachers to be effective evaluators. They include the ability to (1) analyze evaluative information and (2) make judgments regarding evaluative information.

Attention to the development and refinement of preinstructional, instructional, and postinstructional teaching skills is important to all professional educators. Without these skills teachers can never maximize their teaching effectiveness.

Answer Keys

TASK 1.1   Listing the Planning Steps

Step 1 Determining content

Step 2 Writing objectives

Step 3 Planning introduction

Step 4 Selecting instructional strategy

Step 5 Planning closure

Step 6 Planning evaluation

Step 7 Redetermining content

TASK 1.2   Identifying the Planning Steps

1. *Step 3* Planning the introduction
2. *Step 2* Writing the instructional objectives
3. *Step 6* Planning the evaluation
4. *Step 4* Selecting the teaching strategy
5. *Steps 1 and 7* Determining or redetermining content

TASK 1.3   Identifying Teaching Skills

1. G All teachers must have a knowledge of the learning process.
2. G Handling discipline problems is an important aspect of classroom management.
3. G Making observations is important to all teachers.

4. *E*　The major responsibility for teaching reading belongs to elementary teachers. However, current trends are for increased emphasis on secondary level reading.

5. *G*　Listening is an important part of the communication process.

6. *S*　Content knowledge is required only of secondary teachers. However, current trends are for greater emphasis on subject matter acquisition for elementary teachers.

7. *G*　Writing instructional objectives is a skill needed by all teachers.

8. *S*　Generally only secondary teachers work with adolescents. However, since some elementary teachers now teach in middle and junior high schools, these teachers too need training in working with adolescents.

9. *G*　All teachers must be able to close a lesson.

10. *G*　Nonverbal communication is a component of the communication process.

ACTIVITIES

1. *Teacher roles*　Interview several teachers at different grade levels about their roles as educators. Do the teachers feel there is often too much to do? Do they often feel overwhelmed with the paperwork? Do they feel it is important to have good human relations skills?

2. *Classroom observations*　Observe several teachers in an elementary and secondary learning environment. Make a list of the teaching skills observed in both the elementary and the secondary settings. Compare the two lists. Do you note skills applicable only to the elementary setting? the secondary setting? Do you note any skills that apply to both settings?

3. *Self-analysis*　Make a list of personal traits you possess that will assist you in teaching at your grade level. If you are a future or experienced secondary teacher, compare your list with a future or experienced elementary teacher, or vice versa. Are there differences? In what areas do differences exist?

4. *Planning*　Visit with several teachers at different grade levels. Discuss their planning process including the degree of detail they include in their plans. Do they follow the seven-step process presented in this chapter or a modification of the plan? Are teachers at different levels given the same planning time?

REFERENCES

Bruner, J. S. (1966). *Toward a Theory of Instruction*. New York: W. W. Norton.

Charles, C. M. (1985). *Building Classroom Discipline*, 2d ed. New York: Longman.

Clark, L. H., and Starr, I. S. (1986). *Secondary and Middle School Teaching Methods*, 5th ed. New York: Macmillan.

Cooper, J. M., et al. (1986). *Classroom Teaching Skills*, 3d ed. Lexington, Mass.: D. C. Heath.

Jacobsen, D., Eggen, P., Kauchak, D., and Dulaney, C. (1985). *Methods for Teaching: A Skills Approach*. Columbus, Ohio: Charles E. Merrill.

Johansen, J. H., Collins, H. W., and Johnson, J. A. (1986). *American Education: An Introduction to Education*, 5th ed. Dubuque, Iowa: W. C. Brown.

Joyce, B., and Weil, M. (1980). *Models of Teaching*, 2d ed. Englewood Cliffs, N. J.: Prentice-Hall.

Montague, E. J. (1987). *Fundamentals of Secondary Classroom Instruction*. Columbus, Ohio: Charles E. Merrill.

Making Systematic Observations

After completing your study of Chapter 2, you should be able to:

1. Compare and contrast nonsystematic and systematic observation

2. Differentiate among the three common types of data

3. State two reasons why it is important to be able to differentiate among different types of data

4. Differentiate between objective data and subjective data

5. Contrast frequency measure, duration measure, and time-sample measure

6. Explain the purposes of systematic observation

7. Identify procedures an observer should follow in making systematic observations

8. Apply systematic observation techniques to an observational experience

9. Write accurate, objective reports of observational experiences

10. Describe and use various classroom interaction observational techniques

As a classroom teacher, your professional responsibilities include being both an active participant and an observer in a dynamic learning environment. As an active participant, you are a member of an ongoing social process, you plan and implement various educational programs, and you develop and implement a variety of instructional activities. As an observer, you are required to continuously collect information for both planning and management.

Accurate observations should help you answer questions such as: Am I asking enough questions? Should I plan more activities to teach this concept? Are the students ready to go on to the next unit? Is my seating arrangement appropriate? Are students staying on task?

BENEFITS OF OBSERVATION

The information you collect as an observer can be used to analyze student learning, the learning environment, and student attitudes toward learning and schooling. Based on these analyses, you will make certain conclusions about your teaching effectiveness and the progress your students are making academically and socially. These conclusions will then form the basis for the next phase of instructional planning. Reteaching may be necessary.

You can also collect information about student behavior and learning during the instructional process itself. This information will provide the ongoing feedback needed for classroom management and on-the-spot instructional adjustments, such as whether or not to terminate an activity, to use more examples, to provide more hands-on experiences, or to stop instruction and determine who is causing the disruption at the back of the room. The accuracy and effectiveness of these decisions will be directly related to the validity of your observations. Thus, when your observational skills are highly developed, you will know almost automatically what to do.

Finally, teachers who observe their own behavior can analyze the effectiveness of their teaching behaviors. For example, a teacher might ask: "Am I asking enough questions?" "Is my use of reinforcement effective?" "Do I dominate my class discussions?" "How do I react to different students?" With an understanding of information collection techniques and a conceptual and theoretical framework for analyzing teacher and student classroom behaviors, these questions can be answered. Thus, teachers who occasionally (about once a month) tape and analyze their lessons can often improve their teaching effectiveness.

TYPES OF CLASSROOM OBSERVATION

There are basically two types of classroom observation: nonsystematic and systematic. With nonsystematic observation the observer or teacher simply watches and takes note of the behaviors, characteristics, and personal interactions that seem significant. Nonsystematic classroom observation tends to be anecdotal and subjective.

With systematic classroom observation, the observer typically measures the frequency, duration, magnitude, or latency of specific behaviors or events. However, since classroom interaction is complex and fast paced, it is difficult to record every instance of a targeted occurrence. For example detecting which student disrupted a group activity or recited incorrectly during a group recitation would be difficult to observe.

One of the greatest obstacles to becoming an effective observer is the danger of misinterpreting what you see. Everyone has past experiences and biases that can easily distort what he or she sees. The concepts and systematic observation techniques presented in this chapter will help you overcome these problems.

TYPES OF DATA

Systematically collected data are valuable only when they are used to improve the instructional process. Thus, the specific kinds of data needed will depend on what aspects of teacher or student behavior you are studying. A brief introduction to the major types of data and their instructional uses follows.

Valued data are "data that involve the judgment of an observer" (Hansen, 1977, p. 351). That is, the observer makes a value judgment regarding the observed behavior or event. For example, having observed the number of questions asked by the teacher, the teacher's use of movement or reinforcement, or student time on task, the observer then makes a subjective statement regarding what was observed. Thus, following the observation, the observer might record "The number of questions asked by the teacher was appropriate," or "The teacher used movement effectively, " or "The teacher didn't use enough reinforcement," or "The teacher was ineffective at keeping students on task." Valued data, then, are nothing more than subjective value judgments on the part of the observer and are useful only when the observer's value judgments can be trusted to be consistent with tested techniques for effective teaching. For teachers seeking to improve their day-to-day instruction, this may mean taking notes on their own teaching skills or on student behaviors and making judgments regarding how appropriate they are. However, when the behaviors being observed are complex or when judgments external to the learning environment are to be made, descriptive or reproduced data must be collected.

Descriptive data are "data that have been organized, categorized, or quantified by an observer but do not involve a value judgment" (Hansen, 1977, p. 352). This type of data demands that the observer decide which behavioral category (if any) an observed behavior belongs to. It also means counting the number of times a specific behavior is observed. For example, the observer might classify teacher questions as divergent or convergent, or classify teacher reinforcement statements as positive or negative, or label student movement as being necessary or unnecessary, or decide which teacher statements represent encouragement and record all such cases. Once recorded, a judgment must be made regarding the appropriateness of the observed behaviors. This judgment can be made by the observer, the teacher, or by other interested individuals. The value of descriptive data is related to the observer's expertise in recognizing and categorizing specific behaviors and then evaluating their appropriateness, that is, in turning descriptive data into valued data.

Reproduced data have been recorded in video, audio, or total transcript (verbatim) form and can be reproduced when desirable (Hansen, 1977, p. 354). The data include a total reproduction of the targeted environment or behaviors. With this type of data collection, the observer might decide to record behaviors in the form of a list. Thus, the observer's record might consist of a list (verbatim) of teacher statements or student questions or a list or diagram of the teacher's movement during a lesson. The data are valued only when the observer can be trusted to operate the equipment properly or to record the observed behaviors accurately. When data from verbatim reproductions are eventually extracted and used, they inevitably fall into one of the other two categories. Therefore, reproduced data will not be addressed further; you need only refine your skill in recording descriptive and valued data.

There are two important reasons for learning to differentiate between the two types of data. First, it seems likely that future teachers will increasingly observe one another in action. As more states and school districts implement minimum teaching competencies and adopt master teacher and career ladder plans (Zumwalt, 1985), inexperienced and less proficient teachers will be allowed to observe master teachers. Likewise, master teachers will be given the opportunity to observe and provide constructive feedback to fellow teachers. With this in mind, it is important to be able to interpret the observational language used by supervisors and other teachers who observe in your classroom.

Both descriptive and valued data can help you examine, refine, and modify your teaching skills. You need only decide which type is most useful for the purposes of the observation. You may collect one type of information for planning purposes or to provide the feedback you need during instruction and still another type to provide feedback to colleagues. Now try your skill in classifying the two types of data by completing Task 2.1.

TASK 2.1   Classifying Data

Classify the following recorded data statements as being valued data (V) or descriptive data (D). Check your responses with those given at the end of the chapter.

_____ 1. The teacher used a student idea four times in the 50-minute period.

_____ 2. The lesson was appropriate for the class.

_____ 3. The teacher did not provide sufficient examples for the development of the concept.

_____ 4. The teacher used too much verbal reinforcement and not enough nonverbal reinforcement.

_____ 5. The same student, Cindi, answered five teacher questions.

_____ 6. The set induction activity for the lesson was appropriate.

_____ 7. The teacher used the lecture method for 20 minutes and the discussion method for 30 minutes in this lesson.

_____ 8. The teacher is effective at using wait time.

We look, but do we really see? Observing, especially in an objective way, is difficult to learn since it requires detachment. Too often we tend to include our own feelings, attitudes, and biases in what we observe. Therefore, inasmuch as the ability to make objective observations is a relatively unrefined skill for most novice teachers and for many experienced ones, it is a skill that must be developed and practiced. We shall now take a closer look at making systematic observations.

SYSTEMATIC OBSERVATION

Observations can, if made correctly, provide highly accurate, detailed, verifiable information not only about students and your own teaching but also about the context in which the observations are made. However, you must always keep in mind that behavior is complex and is the product of many interrelated causes. Those who observe human behavior can easily draw false conclusions (Cartwright and Cartwright, 1974). Specific skills and techniques that will help you study and analyze the teaching-learning environment in a systematic and objective fashion become essential for effective teaching. These skills will help you become more aware of and better prepared to control both your own and student behaviors and will ultimately lead to increased learning. Those parts of the learning environment that can be observed, classified, and controlled are the ones that can be used to facilitate learning.

Scientific observers not only acquire more accurate information than do casual observers, but they also apply what they learn more effectively because they follow certain procedures. Although observers who have developed their observation skills make special efforts to be unbiased and objective, even those who are highly trained tend to be selective in what they see. That is, everyone chooses which behaviors or actions to pay attention to and which to ignore. For example, teachers often ignore the negative behaviors of their better students while responding to the same behaviors on the part of poorer students.

Given any situation, a wide range of observations is possible. No observer can monitor everything that takes place in a classroom because classroom environments are just too complex. For instance, if you are recording the interactions in a reading group, it would be difficult to record accurately all the behaviors occurring in the rest of the classroom. One way to overcome this difficulty is to observe only a small group (such as the reading group) or the behavior of only a few students. The target group can be studied intensively, and their behavior will often mirror what takes place in the total classroom.

Another focusing strategy is to limit the number of behaviors you look for at one time (five or fewer in the beginning). This is an especially useful technique for beginning observers or for teachers participating in self-evaluation. One simply cannot record data during the act of teaching. Audio or video recorders can be extremely useful in such situations since they permit repeated observation. Beginners should probably concentrate on the same behaviors for several days at a time.

Developing an observational plan is necessary if you are to make accurate recordings within an observational setting. Systematic observation represents such a plan in that it provides a useful means of identifying, studying, classifying, and measuring specific interacting variables within the learning environment. Systematic observation requires that you develop specific observational skills, such as the ability to:

1. Differentiate between objective and subjective data

2. Determine the setting in which the behavior will be observed

3. Determine the method for observing and recording the targeted behaviors or events

4. Determine the interval of time the environment will be observed

Individual plans may differ with respect to these elements, resulting in totally different observations. However they may differ, some type of systematic observation plan is needed in order to generate the kind of reliable data needed for instructional improvement.

Objectivity in Observation

Behavior can be defined as "that which is observable and overt; it has to be seen and it should be countable" (Tillman et al., 1975, p. 262). It is impossible to be completely objective in the collection of behavioral data. The very decision of what to record, what not to record, or how to categorize the information involves subjective judgments. Thus, being objective does not mean discounting your feelings, attitudes, and thoughts; it simply means using them to produce data that is objective. You should always strive to record what is actually happening rather than what you think is happening and your interpretation of it.

The context surrounding behavior should also be observed, for very often it will be useful when drawing inferences and conclusions and arriving at decisions. You should think broadly about all behaviors in the observational setting and include in your collection of data such items as time, place, the people involved, and objects in the environment.

Good observation then involves selective interpretations of behavior as well as explicit descriptions of specific, observable acts. To avoid erroneous interpretations, the distinction between observable acts (behaviors) and **inferences** (interpretations of behaviors) must be kept in mind. Consider the following statements:

1. Terri likes to read.

2. Joe is a nasty child.

3. Robert is a good student.

4. Mary is very creative.

None of these statements describes overt, observable behavior. Terms such as *likes, nasty, good,* and *creative* are open to interpretation; they are really interpretive conclusions or inferences rather than objective happenings. Objectivity requires specifying the behaviors that lead to such subjective interpretations. For example, Terri may have asked to read aloud in class, which then led you to conclude that she likes to read. Also, terms such as *hot, cold, humid,* and so on are concepts that are in the eyes of the beholder. What is hot or cold to one person may not be to another.

Observations must be objective if they are to be of value. Compare the following statements with those just cited:

1. Terri read five books this month.

2. Joe kicked and hit three other children today at recess.

3. Robert made no errors on his math and English examinations.

4. Mary wrote two stories for the school paper this year.

Note that these observations are overt, observable behaviors which can be counted. They could lead to the inferences and conclusions stated earlier.

Task 2.2 will further develop your skill at differentiating between overt, observable behaviors and inferences and conclusions. Remember that observable behaviors should be countable, whereas inferences are interpretations of behavior.

Even though you cannot always see a process or a characteristic directly, you can often make a reasonable judgment about whether or not it exists based on the behaviors of an individual. What you do is make an inference about the presence or absence of certain characteristics and processes based on behavioral evidence. This supporting evidence must be observable so that others can review it and decide whether or not they agree with your inference.

You must always be careful in drawing inferences and conclusions because you can never be absolutely sure they are accurate. For example you cannot be sure of inferences you might make when you hear Tommy say, "I really like school!" Is Tommy saying this because he thinks you want to hear it? You can never be completely sure. Therefore, a major concern should be to maintain constant vigilance regarding the question: What behaviors constitute "reasonable" support for the inferences or conclusions being made?

Even though you can never be absolutely sure of the inferences you make, their justification increases in proportion to the observable behaviors supporting them. Observers who habitually make

TASK 2.2 Differentiating between Observations and Inferences

The following is a list of observational statements. Some of the statements are observable behaviors and others are inferences. Check the appropriate category next to each entry. Check your responses with those given at the end of the chapter.

	Behavior	Inference
1. Harry is lazy.	___	___
2. Johnny threw his book.	___	___
3. Mike closed the door.	___	___
4. May had tears in her eyes.	___	___
5. Darrell is very shy around adults.	___	___
6. Pam is easily influenced by other children.	___	___
7. David dropped his pencil.	___	___
8. Al is hyperactive.	___	___
9. James likes to play baseball and football.	___	___
10. Paul acts strange in physical education.	___	___
11. Nickie sat down.	___	___
12. Joyce handed in her homework assignment.	___	___
13. Frank likes any kind of music.	___	___
14. Helen acts in an intelligent manner.	___	___
15. Alan appears neurotic most of the time.	___	___

inferences based on little behavioral data are not carrying out the role and responsibilities of a trained professional. These same observers too often make unsupported instructional decisions.

The Setting

In most instances the setting for your observations will be limited to the classroom or the school grounds. However, as a visiting observer you may only be interested in a limited part of another classroom. For example you may only want information pertaining to a specific classroom group or class activity. However, even when limiting the focus of your observation, you should include environmental data that might influence the targeted behavior. Such things as holidays, temperature, weather, and so forth will often affect observed behavior.

Recording Data

Observational data should be coded in a manner that is easy to record and use. There is no observational system that is suitable for all situations. Symbols can often be used to represent specific behaviors, and they can be recorded on seating charts or other convenient forms such as is shown in Figure 2.1. The particular system used to record data should be simple and tailor-made to the specific observation. For example if only one behavior is being observed, you might use a simple X on your seating chart to record it. Simplicity in the recording of data is especially important

FIGURE 2.1 Recorded Data for Classroom Observation. The circle represents the teacher and the squares represent the students.

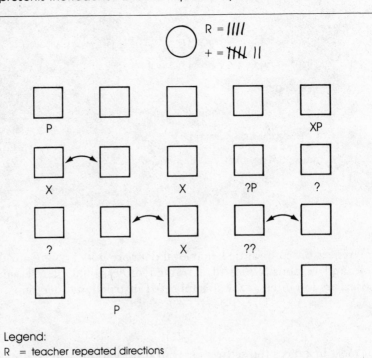

Legend:
R = teacher repeated directions
+ = teacher used reinforcement
P = student needed help
? = student asked question
X = student at board
⌢ = students talked without permission

when you must make observations as you teach. However, as mentioned earlier, when many behaviors are to be recorded or when the behaviors are complex, it is best to use an audio, video, or outside observer to collect data. Table 2.1 lists examples of symbols that should prove useful in recording data.

Behavorial data can also be recorded using different types of measures, such as frequency, duration, or time sample. **Frequency measurement** is employed when you want to determine the number of times certain behaviors are exhibited in a specified length of time. You simply keep a tally of the number of times the behaviors are exhibited.

Duration and time-sample measurements involve data that may not be discrete. That is, it may involve behaviors that continue for a length of time or that take some time to occur.

Duration measurement involves either the length of time a specific behavior continues or the time needed for its occurrence following a given direction or signal. The time a student plays with a disallowed object, or the time it takes for students to turn to the correct page in a book would be examples of duration measurement.

Time-sample measurement is used to sample behavior at predetermined time intervals, such as 5 minutes or 15 minutes. The

TABLE 2.1   Recording Symbols.

LABEL	SYMBOL	DEFINITION
Male	M	Individual is male.
Female	F	Individual is female.
Student Behaviors		
Correct response	+	Student answered correctly.
Wrong response	−	Student answered incorrectly.
No response	0	Student did not answer.
Inappropriate response	=	Student made inappropriate verbal response.
Student disruptive	D	Student caused problem in class.
Teacher Behaviors		
Reinforcement	+	Teacher used positive reinforcement.
Criticize	−	Teacher criticized student behavior.
Question	?	Teacher asked question.
No response	0	Teacher ignored student question or behavior.

behavior can be continuous or discrete. You simply check for the behavior at the end of the specified time interval. For example you might want to check whether students are on task at five-minute intervals and make a record of those who are and those who are not.

Observation Time

The time when data is to be collected is usually determined by the teaching-learning situation and the type of data. If you are an observer in another teacher's classroom and are looking at teacher behavior during instruction, the data should not be collected during seatwork or independent study periods. However, in making general observations, you will be interested in all aspects of behavior in the environment for a specified period. For most purposes, 45 minutes appears to be an adequate period for a representative sampling of behaviors in the learning environment.

You should also keep in mind that your presence in a classroom as a visitor may influence some behaviors within the observational setting. This influence, in general, usually tends to decrease over time. Therefore, it is wise to spend some time in the setting before making observations.

ARRANGEMENTS FOR OBSERVATION

Observations made without a definite purpose or preconceived plan can be both tiresome and unprofitable. Although such unplanned experiences might be interesting, even entertaining to the novice observer, over any length of time the whole experience can become an ordeal. These unplanned observation experiences are generally nothing more than a "look and see" exercise with a "catch what you can" outcome. However, if you are prepared for the observational experience, know what is to be accomplished, and are equipped with the correct techniques, you can obtain valuable firsthand information. But to understand what is to be accomplished and to learn the necessary techniques require that at least two basic conditions are met.

First, you need to know exactly what behaviors to observe in order to achieve the intended purpose. Moreover, you need to know how to use the information once it is obtained. Second, in order to develop a plan of action for the observation, you need to be able to see behaviors as both separate, discrete phenomena and as interactive within the dynamics of the observational site. These two conditions are discussed in the following section.

To get to the heart of what is happening in an observational setting, you must give your full attention, something that is not easy.

Making objective observations is so strenuous in fact, that you can generally only do it for short periods. There will be times when you will want reasons and meanings behind what is happening, and so if possible, exact wording will be recorded. At other times voice quality, body posture, facial expressions, or gestures should be noted. Whatever data is needed, the use of systematic observation techniques will greatly enhance the recording of the data.

WRITING BEHAVIORAL DESCRIPTIONS

Writing a behavioral description of your observations is a difficult task, but it is a prerequisite to making accurate assessments of the learning environment. Tillman, Bersoff, and Dolly (1976) offer the following guidelines:

1. Focus only on those behaviors related to or affecting the situation you are observing.

2. Record, whenever possible, everything that happens in the immediate environment. Attempt to report all conversation verbatim.

3. Report all behaviors sequentially.

4. State descriptions of behavior in a positive way. Avoid stating what did not take place.

5. Try not to report more than one behavioral observation in a sentence, except discrete, short, sequential behaviors.

6. Keep a running account of the actual times of behavioral observations.

7. Do not make interpretations of behavior. Record all observations in standard English and do not theorize.

Attention to the suggested guidelines should improve the accuracy of your observations as a visiting observer or as a teacher in your own classroom. To improve your accuracy even further, an observation form, such as the Site Observation Record Form shown at the end of this chapter, can be used to record data. This form allows you to record recurring behavior with a minimum of record-keeping time. You simply record a behavior the first time it occurs, or prerecord the targeted behaviors, and then tally each occurrence in the frequency column. However, it is essential that a precise description of the collected observations be written immediately following the session. Since descriptions hastily written during the observation are often imprecise, it is best to write them in a more formal manner afterward. This point is especially important if the observations are made as you teach. The guidelines described earlier should be used in writing a formal observation report on a form such as the Behavioral Description Form shown at the end of the chapter.

If the dynamics of classroom life are the object of analysis, a technique known as interaction analysis is quite useful. Before we conclude our discussion of observation, we shall take a brief look at this technique.

CLASSROOM INTERACTION

Teaching is not, as some critics and teachers seem to think, just a matter of teachers' talking and students' listening. Effective teaching involves interactive communication patterns that are skillfully directed. Thus, observers and teachers should be interested in looking at and analyzing classroom interaction patterns. From such an analysis, one can learn whether or not a class is teacher dominated or pupil dominated, open or repressive, and whether the teaching style is direct (student freedom to respond is minimized) or indirect (student freedom to respond is maximized). A detailed description of such an analysis can be found in the Amidon, Casper, and Flanders (1985) training manual.

There are a number of methods for looking at classroom interaction. They vary from simple to complex, with many requiring the services of either an observer or a recorder (audio or video).

Even though the simpler schemes are not as useful as the more sophisticated methods, they can be helpful in detecting glaring faults in the use of various teaching skills. The simplest of these methods calls for the observer to tally each instance of teacher and student talk as, for example, T T P P T T T P T T T P P T T T T T P T. Although this record shows how often the teacher talks compared to the students, it does not reveal how long each talked. A somewhat more sophisticated form of this method is for the observer to sit at the back of the room and record on a form such as that shown in Figure 2.2 the number of times each person speaks. Often the class seating chart can be used to record the data. The disadvantage here is that an outside observer is needed.

The two techniques just described can be refined to yield more information by having the observer record who is talking at regular intervals, about every three or five seconds. This variation has the advantage of telling you who is interacting, how often they interact, and approximately how long each person speaks.

One of the more sophisticated and best known interaction analysis techniques is the Flanders analysis system (Amidon, Casper,

FIGURE 2.2   A Simple Form of Interaction Analysis.   The circle represents the teacher and the squares represent the students.

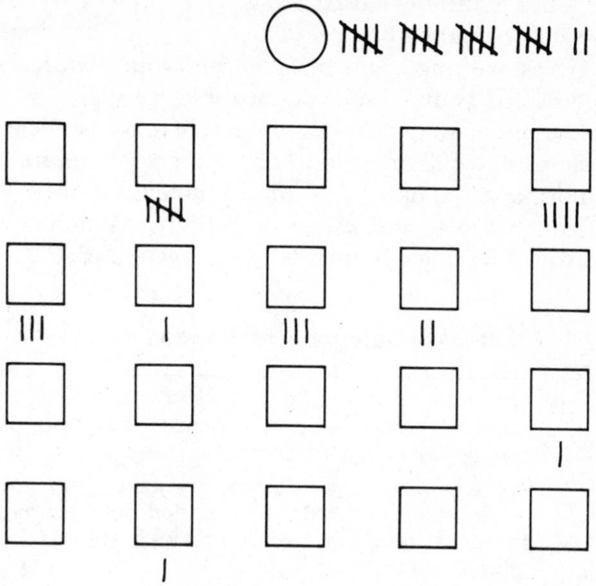

and Flanders, 1985). This system is commonly taught to teachers,
supervisors, and counselors who want to view typical patterns of
verbal exchange in the classroom. The Flanders Interaction Analysis System is concerned only with verbal behavior. It is assumed
that classroom verbal behaviors give an adequate sampling of the
total classroom behaviors. In the Flanders system, classroom verbal interaction is divided into the 10 categories listed in Figure 2.3.
By memorizing and practicing the code, the observer need only
write down a single number to represent a type of verbal activity.
To conduct an observation and analysis, the observer records the
category of action in the classroom every three seconds or whenever a change in category occurs. Then at the conclusion of the
observation, the observer arranges the records into a 10 by 10
matrix for further analysis. A detailed analysis of the matrix
reveals the dynamics of the classroom and the general classroom
atmosphere. By using this system, a teacher or observer can draw
conclusions about the classroom climate and make inferences
about the communication strategies fostered in the classroom.

   The Flanders system is a complex technique. Therefore, some
observers use a simplified version. In this version the observer
records the interaction going on in the classroom on a form such

as that shown in Figure 2.4, but does not arrange the tallies in a matrix. The simplified version does not give as clear a view of the classroom as does the complete system.

The Flanders Interaction Analysis System gives you an excellent overview of the verbal interaction in your classroom, which should give some important insights into your own teaching. If you tape-record your class, it is possible to apply the analysis without the use of an outside observer. There is insufficient space in this chapter to fully develop the Flanders procedure, but detailed information about it and matrix analysis can be found in the Amidon, Casper, and Flanders Training Manual (see references). Now take a few moments to complete Task 2.3.

FIGURE 2.3 Summary of Categories for Flanders Interaction Analysis.

Teacher Talk — Indirect Influence	1.	*Accepts feeling:* accepts and clarifies the feeling tone of the students in a nonthreatening manner. Feelings may be positive or negative. Predicting or recalling feelings is included.
	2.	*Praises or encourages:* praises or encourages student action or behavior. Jokes that release tension, but not at the expense of another individual; nodding head, or saying "um hm?" or "go on" are included.
	3.	*Accepts or uses ideas of students:* clarifying, building, or developing ideas suggested by a student. As teacher brings more of his own ideas into play, shift to Category 5.
	4.	*Asks questions:* asking a question about content or procedure with the intent that a student answer.
Teacher Talk — Direct Influence	5.	*Lecturing:* giving facts or opinions about content or procedures; expressing his own ideas, asking rhetorical questions.
	6.	*Giving directions:* directions, commands, or orders with which a student is expected to comply.
	7.	*Criticizing or justifying authority:* statements intended to change student behavior from nonacceptable to acceptable pattern; bawling someone out; stating why the teacher is doing what he is doing; extreme self-reference.
Student Talk	8.	*Student talk—reponse:* talk by students in response to teacher. Teacher initiates the contact or solicits student statements.
	9.	*Student talk—initiation:* talk by students, which they initiate. If "calling on" student is only to indicate who may talk next, observer must decide whether student wanted to talk. If he did, use this category.
	10.	*Silence or confusion:* pauses, short periods of silence, and periods of confusion in which communication cannot be understood by the observer.

SOURCE: Amidon, E. J., Casper, I. G., and Flanders, N. A. (1985), *The Role of the Teacher in the Classroom: A Manual for Understanding and Improving Teacher Classroom Behavior,* 3d ed. St. Paul, Minn.: Paul S. Amidon, p. 8. Reprinted by permission.

FIGURE 2.4 Simplified Version of Flanders Form.

CATEGORY			TALLIES
Teacher Talk	Indirect	1. Accepts feelings	
		2. Praises or encourages	
		3. Accepts or uses ideas of students	
		4. Asks questions	
	Direct	5. Lectures	
		6. Gives directions	
		7. Criticizes or justifies authority	
Student Talk		8. Student response	
		9. Student initiation	
		10. Silence or confusion	

TASK 2.3 Making Observations

Answer the following questions dealing with the observational process. Check your answers with those given at the end of the chapter.

1. With practice it is possible to be completely objective in making observations.   (True/False)

2. One should always develop a plan of action related to what to observe and how it is to be recorded prior to making an observation. (True/False)

3. One can never be absolutely sure that an inference is correct. (True/False)

4. A recording of the time it takes for a student to be seated after being told to do so is an example of time-sample measurement. (True/False)

5. An observer should write a precise description of an observation as soon as possible after making the observation.   (True/False)

6. Observers should never include their own interpretations in observational data.   (True/False)

7. All classroom interaction schemes require the use of an outside observer to carry out the observation and analysis.   (True/False)

8. Utilization of the Flanders Interaction System requires that one memorize and practice a set of behavior categories before attempting an observation.   (True/False)

ETHICAL CONSIDERATIONS

We must address one final issue before concluding this chapter: the confidentiality of observation information. Statements about observational information should never be made in front of unqualified personnel. Observation information should only be discussed with people on a need-to-know basis. It is equally important to refrain from talking about any observations or other school business outside the school, no matter how great the temptation. Talking to colleagues about observations or behaviors in public places is also professionally unethical.

SUMMARY

Teachers are required to make continuous judgments and decisions about the learning process. They make judgments regarding what to teach next, how to best teach it, who needs extra help, what material to use, and so forth. They make decisions during instruction regarding changes in the planned lesson, pacing of the lesson, management of the lesson, and so forth. The validity of these judgments and decisions depends to a large extent on the ability to make accurate observations. Therefore, skill at being an observer and making valid observations is essential for teachers.

Systematic observation will improve your ability to make valid observations. Using it depends on the following subskills: (1) the ability to collect the type of data best suited for the purpose of the observation, (2) the ability to differentiate between behaviors and inferences, and (3) the ability to plan for the observational experience with respect to the setting to be observed, the recording of data, and the observational time. In addition the writing of accurate behavioral reports will greatly assist you in reaching accurate, final conclusions.

Learning comes best through interaction. Thus, it would be wise to periodically look at your classroom interaction using one of the many observational schemes available. The best known and most commonly used technique of interaction analysis is the Flanders Interaction Analysis System.

Attention to the observation techniques covered in this chapter should make you a better observer, and thus a better teacher.

SITE OBSERVATION RECORD FORM

Observer _____ Date _____

Site_____

Grade/Subject _____ Time: from _____ to _____

Description of observed environment. _____

_____

_____

_____

_____

_____

List all observed behaviors during the observation period. If the same behavior occurs more than once, indicate it by marking tallies in the frequency column.

Observed Behavior   **Frequency**

_____   _____

_____   _____

_____   _____

_____   _____

_____   _____

_____   _____

_____   _____

_____   _____

_____   _____

_____   _____

_____   _____

_____   _____

_____   _____

_____   _____

_____   _____

_____   _____

_____   _____

BEHAVIORAL DESCRIPTION FORM

Name of Recorder _____ Date _____

Site of Observation _____

Grade/Subject _____ Time: from _____ to _____

Describe, in observable terms, the environment within which the observation took place.

_____

_____

_____

_____

_____

_____

Describe, in behavioral terms, behaviors observed during observation session.

_____

_____

_____

_____

_____

_____

_____

_____

_____

_____

_____

_____

_____

_____

_____

_____

TASK 2.1 Classifying Data

1. *D* The observer simply recorded the number of times student ideas were used.

2. *V* The subjective value judgment of "appropriateness" made by the observer.

3. *V* Value judgment of "insufficient" made by the observer.

4. *V* "Too much" and "not enough" are value judgments.

5. *D* The observer recorded the number of questions answered by a student.

6. *V* The subjective value judgment "appropriate" made by the observer.

7. *D* The observer simply recorded the methods used and the time.

8. *V* "Effectiveness" is a value judgment.

TASK 2.2 Differentiating between Observations and Inferences

1. *Inference* "Lazy" is open to interpretation.

2. *Behavior* Observable action.

3. *Behavior* Observable action.

4. *Behavior* Observable action.

5. *Inference* "Shy" is open to interpretation.

6. *Inference* "Easily influenced" is a conclusion.

7. *Behavior* Observable action.

8. *Inference* "Hyperactive" is open to interpretation.

9. *Inference* "Likes" is a conclusion.

10. *Inference* "Strange" is open to interpretation.

11. *Behavior* Observable action.

12. *Behavior* Observable action.

13. *Inference* "Likes" is a conclusion.

14. *Inference* "Intelligent" is open to interpretation.

15. *Inference* "Neurotic" is open to interpretation.

TASK 2.3 Making Observations

1. *False* No amount of practice can make one completely objective.

2. *True* You cannot possibly observe and record everything that happens in a classroom. Therefore, you must decide on what to look for and plan a simple way to record it. A plan will result in more accurate information.

3. *True*   No matter how much positive data is collected, there is always a possibility that an inference could be false.

4. *False*   This is an example of duration measurement.

5. *True*   A precise description should be written as soon as possible so important information is not lost.

6. *False*   Care should be taken in interpreting behaviors, but some interpretation is often helpful in drawing insight regarding the interactions of the classroom.

7. *False*   Teachers can utilize most of the schemes. However, training is often desirable for proper utilization of the more complex forms.

8. *True*   Utilization of the Flanders system requires that a category be recorded every three seconds or that every change in category be recorded. Thus, the categories must be memorized and practiced for the observer to be proficient.

ACTIVITIES

1. *Observation of present setting*   Using the Observation of Present Setting Worksheet, which follows, record observations of your present setting. Record your observations in the order they are noted and limit the observation time to five minutes. When finished, compare your observations with others who have observed the same setting. Consider the following in your comparisons:
    a. The observations selected: Were they the same or selective?
    b. The sequence of the observations: Were they the same?
    c. The strategy used to make the observations: Was a strategy used by everyone and were the strategies different?

2. *Systematic observations*   Complete several observational activities in different teaching-learning environments. Use the Site Observation Record Form to record your observations. As soon as possible after your visit, write a formal description of the observations using the Behavioral Description Form. Plan the following before you make your observation:
    a. The specific behaviors to be observed
    b. The type of data to be recorded
    c. The type of measure to be employed

3. *Classroom interaction*   Complete several classroom interaction observational activities in different teaching-learning environments. Use various techniques for looking at the different classroom interaction patterns.

OBSERVATION OF PRESENT SETTING WORKSHEET

Setting _____

Date _____   Time: from _____ to _____

Observer _____

Observations in Sequence

1. _____

2. _____

3. _____

4. _____

5. _____

6. _____

7. _____

8. _____

9. _____

10. _____

11. _____

12. _____

13. _____

14. _____

15. _____

16. _____

17. _____

18. _____

19. _____

20. _____

REFERENCES

_____ (1986). *Minimum Criteria for Effective Teaching Performance*. Oklahoma City, Oklahoma: Oklahoma State Department of Education.

Amidon, E. J., Casper, I. G., and Flanders, N. A. (1985). *The Role of the Teacher in the Classroom: A Manual for Understanding and Improving Teacher Classroom Behavior*, 3d ed. St. Paul, Minn.: Paul S. Amidon.

Blackham, G. J., and Silberman, A. (1980). *Modification of Child and Adolescent Behavior*. Belmont, Calif.: Wadsworth.

Boehm, A. E., and Weinberg, R. A. (1977). *The Classroom Observer*. New York: Teachers College Press.

Cartwright, C. A., and Cartwright, G. P. (1974). *Developing Observation Skills*. New York: McGraw Hill.

Clark, L. H., and Starr, I. S. (1986). *Secondary and Middle School Teaching Methods*, 5th ed. New York: Macmillan.

Good, T. L., and Brophy, J. E. (1987). *Looking in Classrooms*, 4th ed. New York: Harper and Row.

Hansen, J. (1977). Observation skills. In *Classroom Teaching Skills: A Handbook*, Cooper, J. M., et al. Lexington, Mass.: D. C. Heath.

Lindgren, H. C. (1980). *Educational Psychology in the Classroom*. New York: Oxford University Press.

Ober, R. L., Bentley, E. L., and Miller, E. (1971). *Systematic Observation of Teaching*. Englewood Cliffs, N. J.: Prentice-Hall.

Peter, L. J. (1975). *Competencies for Teaching: Classroom Instruction*. Belmont, Calif.: Wadsworth.

Stallings, J. A. (1977). *Learning to Look*. Belmont, Calif.: Wadsworth.

Tillman, M., Bersoff, D., and Dolly, J. (1978). *Learning to Teach*. Lexington, Mass.: D. C. Heath.

Zumwalt, K. (1985). The master teacher concept: Implications for teacher education. *Elementary School Journal*, 86, pp. 45–54.

PREINSTRUCTIONAL SKILLS

Summer vacation is over. You are ready to start a new school year in which your students learn and grow academically, emotionally, and socially. But where should you begin? What is needed to make the year a good one? Since planning seems to be a key ingredient in most successful ventures, your first task should be to plan. Without planning to direct your energies and the energies of your students and to mobilize environmental resources, your good intentions may go unrealized.

The purpose of this section is to assist you in becoming a better planner. To do so you must decide where you want to go, the best method of getting there, and whether you have gotten there. Chapter 3 will help you determine where you want to go, that is, with developing your skill at writing well-stated objectives. Chapter 4 shows how to plan presentations that achieve the stated objectives, and Chapter 5 examines the evaluation process.

Writing Objectives

After completing your study of Chapter 3, you should be able to:

1. Define learning

2. Provide valid reasons for stating instructional objectives

3. Define and contrast educational goals, informational objectives, and instructional objectives

4. Compare and contrast overt and covert behavioral changes

5. Name and define the four components that make up a properly written instructional objective

6. Write objectives that include the four components of a well-stated objective

7. Name and describe the three domains of learning

8. Classify given objectives as being cognitive, affective, or psychomotor and rate them as higher or lower level in each domain

9. Prepare (write) educational goals, informational objectives, and instructional objectives at different levels of cognitive, affective, and psychomotor sophistication

Learning can be defined as change in a student's capacity for performance as a result of experience. Effective teaching should, therefore, be directed toward these targeted changes in performance. Thus, in planning instruction you must first decide what changes you want to take place as a result of your instruction, or what will result from your teaching. The intended changes should be specified in your instructional objectives. Viewed in this context, an **objective** can be defined as a clear and unambiguous description of your instructional intent. An objective is not a statement of what you plan to put into the lesson (content), but instead a statement of what your students should get out of the lesson. Thus, your teaching model can be viewed as shown in Figure 3.1.

The model shows that the first task is to establish your objectives. Second, you teach toward the acquisition of the stated objectives using the selected teaching approach. Finally, you evaluate students' attainment of the stated objectives. If students do not achieve the intended objectives, you may either select a different approach or you may alter the original objectives. If students achieve the targeted outcomes, you are ready to go on to the next set of objectives.

VALUE OF OBJECTIVES

Why should you take the time to write objectives? In the first place, as indicated in the preceding teaching model, your teaching approach will be dictated to a large extent by your objectives. These objectives demand certain learning environments and activity sequences. For example if a lesson objective is the acquisition of a specific motor skill, your activities must include practice and refinement of that skill. If, on the other hand, the objective is related to the knowledge of specific muscles one uses in performing certain motor skills, a textbook and related diagrams would probably suffice.

Another important reason for stating objectives is related to the evaluation process. You will not know whether your students have

FIGURE 3.1   Teaching Model.

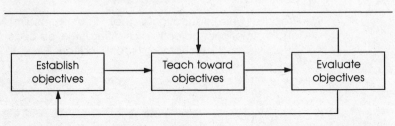

acquired the targeted learning unless you know what you intended to teach and have evaluated that intent. Thus, your objectives set the framework for your evaluation. Of equal importance to the instructional process is the fact that objectives assist you in communicating with your students. When your objectives are shared with the students, and they should always be shared either verbally or in writing, students know what is expected of them. They do not have to guess what is important. They do not have to guess what will be on the test!

In our discussion thus far we have been concerned with stating objectives in terms of specific instructional intent that can be observed and evaluated. However, there are several levels to instructional intent. At the very general, abstract level are statements of the goals that a school might set for its graduates. At the other extreme are very specific statements of what students will be able to do following instruction. Let us now look at the different levels of instructional intent in greater detail.

GOAL AND OBJECTIVE SPECIFICITY

Too often the terms *goals* and *objectives* are incorrectly interchanged. However, there is a difference in the level of specificity at which they should be written. **Goals** are extremely broad statements that are used to describe the purposes of schooling, a course, or a unit of instruction. Objectives, on the other hand, are narrower statements of the intended learning of a unit or specific lesson. Moreover, objectives also vary in the level of specificity depending on the type of objective written.

A nomenclature that differentiates between goals and objectives, as well as between the specificity levels of objectives, has been developed. Unfortunately there is little agreement about how this terminology should be used. The terms *educational goals, educational aims,* and *general objectives* are often used to denote broad general purposes, whereas the terms *specific objectives, informational objectives, behavioral objectives, performance objectives,* and *instructional objectives* are often used to denote the more specific learning targets.

Generally goals and objectives are written at three different levels. In this text we label the three levels, in descending order of specificity, educational goals, informational objectives, and instructional objectives, as depicted in Figure 3.2. In theory and in their proper use, the more specific objectives are subordinate to and are contained in the more general goals. Thus, goals and objectives can be thought of as forming a continuum from general to specific as suggested in Figure 3.2. Educational goals are usually written for a school, course, or unit, followed by (in descending

FIGURE 3.2   General to Specific Continuum for Goals and Objectives.

Most general		Most specific
•————————————	•————————————	•
Educational goals	Informational objectives	Instructional objectives

order) informational and instructional objectives written for specific lessons and exercises. This sequence may vary somewhat depending on the writer. Some writers prefer using a combination of informational and instructional objectives for a unit of study or for specific lessons.

Examples of the three different levels of specificity for goals and objectives from a social studies course are shown in Table 3.1. Note that the specificity increases as you move down through the examples. Thus, informational objectives are subordinate to educational goals, and instructional objectives are subordinate to informational objectives.

EDUCATIONAL GOALS

Educational goals are extremely broad and may take weeks, months, or even years to achieve. Note the broad terms of the goal in Table 3.1. It is the entire intent of the course or unit, that is, what the teacher wishes to accomplish in the broadest possible sense. The informational and instructional objectives then support the educational goal. That is, they tell what the students will do to show

TABLE 3.1   Examples of Goal and Objective Specificity.

TYPE	EXAMPLE
Educational goal	The student will become a knowledgeable citizen.
Informational objective	The student will match major industries to their respective region in the United States.
Instructional objective	Given a list of industries and United States regions, the student will match each industry to its respective region with 90 percent accuracy.

that they have become knowledgeable citizens. Other examples of educational goals are:

1. The student will learn to read.

2. The student will live a healthful life.

3. The student will appreciate art and music.

4. The student will know how to solve algebraic equations.

5. The student will think clearly and rationally.

Note the use of the verbs *learn, live, appreciate, know,* and *think* in the preceding examples. These verbs make the statements vague; they are not stated in observable, measurable terms. In fact they appear to be so vague that they give no help at all in planning instruction. Yet, on closer examination they do set the general direction of instruction and, consequently, are the first step in deciding what to teach. The next step is to decide on the specifics related to these goals. That is, the teacher must now decide in a precise manner exactly what students should know and do to show that they have accomplished the goals. These decisions are then written up as more specific objectives: informational and instructional.

The point of all this is that in planning you must first develop your course goals, then develop informational and instructional objectives. The goals give the general direction to take and also give an overview of what the students will know or be able to do after your instruction. You then state specifically, in observable and measurable terms, exactly what the students will do to show you that you have accomplished your goals. These latter statements make up your informational and instructional objectives.

COVERT VERSUS OVERT BEHAVIOR

The basic purpose of schooling and teaching is to cause students to learn something. Thus, as a result of the instruction, students should act or be inclined to act differently from before. There is a change in the individual. This change can be covert (not easily observed) or overt (observable). Writers of educational goals are concerned with covert, internal changes, which are less clearly measurable than are the behaviors associated with the more specific objectives. Verbs associated with educational goals include *know, understand,* and *appreciate.* Writers of informational and instructional objectives, on the other hand, are concerned with overt, observable behaviors which can be tested and measured. Thus, they tend to use measurable verbs, such as *list, explain,* and *match.*

Educational goals cannot be easily measured or directly observed. They lack the specification of exactly what, in observable terms, the student is to do to show that the intended learning has taken place. Thus, the verbs used in writing educational goals are often rather vague, ambiguous, and open to interpretation.

Table 3.2 lists verbs that are appropriate for writing educational goals (covert) and verbs that are appropriate for writing informational and instructional objectives (overt). Note the difference in clarity of language between the two groups. After carefully studying Table 3.2, complete Task 3.1, which will test your skill at identifying covert (nonobservable) and overt (observable) verbs.

TABLE 3.2   Illustrative Verbs for Writing Goals and Objectives.

COVERT (NONOBSERVABLE) VERBS	OVERT (OBSERVABLE) VERBS	
apply	add	label
appreciate	analyze	list
believe	arrange	locate
comprehend	build	measure
cope	calculate	name
demonstrate	choose	operate
enjoy	circle	order
familiarize	classify	pick
grasp	compare	point
imagine	construct	pronounce
know	contrast	read
like	define	recite
realize	distinguish	select
recognize	draw	sing
think	explain	sort
understand	graph	underline
value	identify	write

TASK 3.1   Identifying Verbs

Given below is a listing of verbs appropriate for writing goals and objectives. Label the listed verbs as being covert (nonobservable) (C) or overt (observable) (O). Check your responses with those given at the end of the chapter.

_____ 1. tell	_____ 4. comprehend	_____ 7. pantomime
_____ 2. place	_____ 5. sing	_____ 8. grasp
_____ 3. design	_____ 6. know	_____ 9. appreciate

If you had trouble with Task 3.1, spend some time studying Table 3.2. We are now ready to look at writing informational and instructional objectives in detail. However, before we do, we shall look at what constitutes a well-stated objective.

WELL-STATED OBJECTIVES

Mager (1984) and Kibler, Barker, and Miles (1970) have developed very influential systems for stating objectives. According to these writers, a well-stated objective should include four components: the performance, a product, the conditions, and the criterion.

The Performance

A well-stated objective must be written in terms of what students are expected to do, not what the teacher is to do. Suppose the following statement had been written for an objective: The teacher will pronounce the new vocabulary words.

It is evident what the teacher is to do, but there is no indication of what the students are to do. Since student learning is the purpose of instruction, well-stated objectives should always be written in terms of observable student performance. Thus, the preceding objective might be restated in this way: The student will pronounce the new vocabulary words.

Special care must also be taken to select the proper verb when writing objectives. Above all the language must be clear. There must be no ambiguity. Each verb in your objective must mean the same to you, an interested colleague, or the principal. Subjective terms, such as *learn, realize,* and *understand,* should not be used as performance verbs in writing objectives. These terms are open to interpretation and might have different meanings to different individuals. Instead use terms that denote observable actions (overt) or behaviors (see Table 3.2). For example your intent might be for students to be able:

To identify (in writing) . . .

To explain (orally) . . .

To list . . .

To construct . . .

Certain verbs represent special cases in terms of our ability to directly view the performance. Verbs such as *identify, distinguish, compare,* and *add* represent internal (covert) processes in that the actions cannot be directly observed. You cannot directly see someone identify, distinguish, compare, or add, but you can see some action that shows that the process has taken place. The action could include such behaviors as circling, pointing, or checking to show identifying; checking, sorting, or writing the descriptions to show distinguishing; listing or writing the characteristics to show comparing; and writing or orally stating the sum to show adding. Mager (1984) calls these observable verbs indicator verbs and suggests that you add an indicator verb to the objective to specify the action when confronted with special covert verbs that cannot be observed directly. Applying this procedure to the verbs cited earlier, the objective could be rewritten as:

The student will identify (circle) . . .

The student will distinguish (check) . . .

The student will compare (in writing) . . .

The student will add (write the sum) . . .

The performance component in a well-stated objective specifies exactly what student actions should be observed as a result of instruction. If the objective verb represents an internal, covert process that might lead to vagueness, you would be wise to add an overt indicator verb for clarity. If, however, you feel the internal, covert process verb is clear and not open to interpretation, there is no need for an indicator verb.

The Product

The product is what students will produce by their action. It is that product which will be evaluated to determine whether the objective has been mastered. The product can be a written sentence, a written sum, listed names, a demonstrated skill, or a constructed object. We list here some statements that contain the first two components of a well-stated objective, the performance and the product. The portion of the statement that has been underlined is the product of the action.

The student will write the numerals to ten.

The student will identify (underline) the nouns in a sentence.

The student will list the main ideas in a short story.

The student will classify leaves into groups based on texture.

The student will solve (write answer) two-digit multiplication algorithms.

The product then is the planned outcome resulting from the instructional process. It is what you want students to produce or be able to do.

The Conditions

Under what conditions will students perform the intended action? Will they be allowed to use an open book? What materials will be used? Where will they perform? These questions are answered in the conditions component of your objective. This component of a well-stated objective includes the information, tools or equipment, and materials that will or will not be available to students; any special limitations or restrictions as to time and space; and any other requirements that may be applicable. Examples of conditions that might be included in a well-stated objective include:

Given a list of 20 authors . . .

After reading chapter 2 . . .

Using the class textbook . . .

Given a ruler and protractor . . .

Without the use of references . . .

. . . on a multiple-choice test . . .

. . . before the class . . .

. . . during a 10-minute interval . . .

. . . from a list of equations . . .

In writing the conditions component of a well-stated objective, you should attempt to visualize under what conditions the students will show mastery and try to duplicate these conditions as nearly as possible in your objective. Some teachers also believe that objectives should always begin with a phrase such as "Upon completion of the lesson (or unit, or course), the student will . . ." because the intended action is to take place only after instruction has been concluded. However, if you keep in mind that the intended action always represents terminal behavior, there is no real need to add the phrase. Whether or not you add the phrase is entirely up to you.

The Criterion

The fourth and last component of a well-stated objective is the level of acceptable student performance. Here you state the level of behavior you will accept as satisfactory or the minimum level for showing mastery. The criterion level may be stated as follows:

As the minimum number acceptable:

. . . at least three reasons . . .

. . . all five steps . . .

As the percent or proportion acceptable:

. . . with 80 percent accuracy . . .

. . . 90 percent of the 20 problems . . .

. . . nine of the ten cases . . .

As an acceptable tolerance:

. . . within ± 10 percent . . .

. . . to the nearest hundredth . . .

. . . correct to the nearest percent . . .

As acceptable limits of time:

. . . within 10 minutes . . .

. . . in less than five minutes . . .

As a combination of acceptable standards:

. . . at least two problems within a five-minute period . . .

. . . within 20 minutes with 90 percent accuracy . . .

Or it may be stated as any other standard of acceptance. Usually your standard is selected on the basis of past experiences and class expectations.

This completes our discussion of the four components of a well-stated objective. Table 3.3 gives a review of these four components. Study the figure and take a few minutes to complete Task 3.2.

TABLE 3.3 Components of a Well-Stated Objective.

PART	QUESTION TO ASK	EXAMPLE
Student performance	Do what?	Write
Product of performance	What is result?	Three sentences
Conditions of performance	Under what conditions?	Given three nouns and three verbs
Performance criterion	How well?	With no more than one error

TASK 3.2   Identifying the Components of Well-Stated Objectives

For each objective given below, circle the performance, bracket the product, underline the conditions once, and underline the criterion twice. Check your answers with those given at the end of the chapter.

1.   Given a set of pictures, the student will be able to place them in proper sequence with no more than one error.

2.   Given the necessary materials and the dimensions, the student will construct a polygon with all dimensions being within 5 percent.

3.   The student will be able to identify (select letter) on a multiple-choice test the subplots of the poems read in class with 100 percent accuracy.

4.   After completing a series of Spanish language tapes, the student will orally recite a given Spanish dialogue with no errors in pronunciation.

5.   The student will write a 300-word essay on a given social studies topic with no sentence fragments and no more than two errors in grammar.

Did you have any trouble with Task 3.2? If not, good work! Number 4 was a little tricky, and you may have included the phrase "a given Spanish dialogue" as part of the conditions. Technically you are correct; however, the dialogue also represents the product which will be evaluated. Therefore, you could have included it in both the conditions and the product.

Now that you know the basic components of a well-written objective, you are ready to differentiate between informational and instructional objectives.

INFORMATIONAL AND INSTRUCTIONAL OBJECTIVES

Informational objectives are abbreviations of instructional objectives. **Instructional objectives** contain all four components of a well-stated objective, but informational objectives specify only the student performance and the product. Consider the following example of an instructional and an informational objective written for the same instructional intent:

Instructional Objective: Given a list of alternatives on a multiple-choice test, the student will select the definitions for the terms *triangle, rectangle, square, trapezoid, circle, rhombus,* and *parallelogram* with 100 percent accuracy. **Informational Objective:** The student will select the definitions for the terms *triangle, rectangle, square, trapezoid, circle, rhombus,* and *parallelogram*.

The informational objective is an abbreviation of the instructional objective in that it omits the conditions (given a list of alternatives on a multiple-choice test) and the criterion for judging minimum mastery (100 percent accuracy). The informational objective contains only the performance (to select) and the products to be selected (definitions for the terms *triangle, rectangle, square, trapezoid, circle, rhombus,* and *parallelogram*). Conditions apply only at the time of assessment and may not always be needed in your objective statement. That is, they will often be standard and understood by students. Likewise, the criterion may not always be needed and may be very artificial in that the mastery level will be determined when the evaluative information is processed.

Most teachers use informational objectives to share their instructional intent with students. In most cases this suffices. However, if more information is needed to communicate the exact intent, you should write instructional objectives or perhaps informational objectives with the conditions or the criterion added.

This concludes our formal discussion of the different types of objectives. Take a few minutes to complete Task 3.3.

TASK 3.3 Objective Concepts

Answer the following questions. Compare your responses with those given at the end of the chapter.

1. List the three benefits derived from the writing of objectives.

   a. _____

   _____

   b. _____

   _____

   c. _____

   _____

2. It is sometimes unwise to share your objectives with students. (True/False)

3. List the nomenclature of learning intent in terms of specificity from least to most.

   a. _____

   b. _____

   c. _____

4. List and describe the four components of a well-stated objective.

a. _____

_____

b. _____

_____

c. _____

_____

d. _____

_____

5. Informational objectives usually contain all four components of a well-stated objective.   (True/False)

CLASSIFICATION OF OBJECTIVES

Objectives are often classified as to the primary type of learning the instruction is trying to accomplish. The most commonly used system for classifying objectives is the taxonomy developed by Bloom (1956) and Krathwohl (1964). This system is divided into three major categories or domains of learning: the cognitive, the affective, and the psychomotor. Each domain is arranged in hierarchical order from simple to complex. In spite of this, each level subsumes the previous level. That is, the objectives at one level make use of and build on behaviors found in the preceding level. Likewise, in reality the domains are interrelated. For example when students are writing (psychomotor), they are also recalling information and thinking (cognitive), and they are likely to have some kind of emotional response to the task.

Cognitive Domain

Objectives in the cognitive domain are concerned with imparting knowledge and thinking skills. The objectives can range from simple recall of information to complex synthesis and the creation of new ideas. This domain is concerned mainly with the subject matter content students are expected to learn.

Some performance verbs (arranged here according to the complexity of response) commonly associated with writing objectives in the cognitive domain include: define, distinguish, identify, restate, explain, infer, apply, use, choose, classify, categorize, write, design, assess, compare, and contrast. Examples of informational and instructional objectives include such statements as:

1. The student will define the terms *common noun* and *proper noun.*

2. The student will explain (in writing) the importance of mathematics in everyday life.

3. The student will design an experiment to test the effect of three different soaps on clothing.

4. Given various classes of music, the student will give (write) at least three effects each type of music has on society.

5. Given a sample of French prose, the student will verbally translate it into English with no more than two errors.

Affective Domain

Objectives in the affective domain are concerned with emotional development. Thus, the affective domain deals with attitudes, feelings, and emotions, and they vary according to the degree of internalization sought.

Since teachers must be concerned with the total development of students, not just their cognitive development, they need to consider attitudes, feelings, and emotions in their instructional planning. Yet most teachers do not, partly because it is difficult to write objectives for the affective domain. The reason for the difficulty is that it is hard to translate attitudes, feelings, and emotions into overt, observable behaviors. For example the affective objective, "The student will like reading," is not properly written. The behavior *like* is not observable. Students must do something observable to show that they like reading. Replace the verb *like* with an observable behavior assumed to indicate liking, for example, "The student will volunteer to read in class." However, volunteering is only one of many possible indicators that the student likes to read. Some performance verbs, arranged from limited internalization to high internalization, often associated with writing objectives in the affective domain include: to freely select, to respond positively to, to listen, to volunteer, to applaud, to support, to argue for (against), to complete, and to rate high (low).

When desired behaviors are related to the affective domain, you must observe the behaviors in a free-choice situation to obtain a true indication of student attitudes and feelings. If the situation is not free choice, students may exhibit the desired behaviors for a reward of some type or because they want to please you. For example the affective objective, "The student will complete all mathematics assignments," would not be appropriate for showing a positive attitude toward mathematics. This objective must be rewritten for a free-choice situation. An example is, "The student will complete optional mathematics assignments with no extra credit given." Another technique often used to reveal attitudes and interests is the administration of attitude and interest inventories. These instruments will be discussed at length in Chapter 5.

To summarize, objectives in the affective domain must be written in overt, observable terms, and the behaviors must take place in free-choice situations. Other examples of informational and instructional objectives in the affective domain include:

1. The student will eagerly participate in class discussions of history-related topics.

2. Given an attitude survey at the beginning and end of the course, the student will rate science higher on the end of course survey.

3. When given the opportunity to select the class reading, the student will freely select poetry at least once during the semester.

4. The student will attend a music concert during the semester without receiving class credit for attendance.

5. Given the opportunity, the student will volunteer to stay after school to care for the classroom plants at least three times during the year.

Psychomotor Domain

Objectives in the psychomotor domain relate to the development of muscular and motor skills and range from beginning to expert performances. Some examples of performance objectives, from simple to complex muscle control, that can be used in writing objectives in the psychomotor domain are: run, walk, measure, construct, type, play, align, and focus. Examples of informational and instructional objectives in the psychomotor domain include:

1. The student will construct a table.

2. The student will type a paragraph.

3. Given a piano and the music, the student will play the piece with no more than two errors.

4. At the end of the year, the student will run a mile in less than eight minutes.

5. Given a meter stick, the student will measure the room within five percent of the correct value.

Most learning in the classroom will contain elements of all three domains. Nevertheless, in writing your objectives, your major emphasis is usually directed toward cognitive, affective, or psychomotor learning. Now try your skill at identifying objectives in the three domains by completing Task 3.4.

TASK 3.4 Identifying the Domain of Objectives

Classify each of the following objectives according to its most prominent behavior: cognitive (C), affective (A), or psychomotor (P). Check your responses with those given at the end of the chapter.

_____ 1. The student will correctly adjust the microscope.

_____ 2. The student will write an essay in which an argument for or against prayer in school is developed.

_____ 3. Given the materials and the picture of a sugar molecule, the student will create a model of a sugar molecule with 100 percent accuracy.

_____ 4. The student will voluntarily check out books related to art.

_____ 5. Given a story, the student will orally read for at least five minutes with no more than four errors.

_____ 6. Given a paragraph, the student will type at a rate of 50 words per minute with fewer than two errors per minute.

_____ 7. The student will argue for more science in the public schools.

_____ 8. The student will correctly write the sums for all the basic addition facts.

_____ 9. Given an attitude inventory, the student will rate social studies on the high end of the scale.

_____ 10. The student will correctly compute (write answer) the volume of a cube, cone, and pyramid.

DOMAIN TAXONOMIES

Although objectives for a given instructional situation can be written at each taxonomic level, Mager (1984) suggests that this is a waste of time and effort. If you have completed a suitable analysis of instructional intent, you know at what level you want your students to learn and thus will automatically write objectives at those levels. There will be no need to write objectives at all levels.

Teachers often fall into the habit of writing objectives only for the lower taxonomic levels since objectives at the higher levels are more difficult to write. A working knowledge of the instructional intent of the various taxonomic levels helps prevent this pitfall. Thus, knowledge of the taxonomies should be used to formulate the best possible objectives for your teaching intent and to ensure that your intent is not overly focused on the lower levels.

A brief overview of the taxonomies for each of the three domains of learning follows. A more detailed description of each can be found by referring to one of the references listed at the end of the chapter. The cognitive taxonomy presented is adapted from the work of Bloom (1956). However, Bloom's two highest levels, synthesis and evaluation, have been combined into a single "creative" level. The affective taxonomy presented here has been adapted from the work of Krathwohl (1964), and it too combines the two highest levels, organization and characterization, into a single level labeled "commitment."

Levels of Cognitive Learning

Learning intent in the cognitive domain ranges from simple recall of facts to complex syntheses of information and the creation of new ideas. As adapted from the work of Bloom (1956), five levels of learning are included in the cognitive learning taxonomy.

1. **Knowledge learning** refers to the simple recall of previously learned materials. This may involve the recall of terminology, basic principles, generalizations, and specific facts, such as dates, events, persons, and places. No manipulation or interpretation of the learned material is required. Knowledge-level objectives can be expressed with such verbs as: identify, define, list, match, write, state, name, label, and describe. Knowledge-level examples include:

The student will spell at least 70 percent of the words in the third grade speller.

The student will list the names of 12 of the last 15 presidents of the United States.

2. **Comprehension** is the lowest level of understanding, and may involve changing the form of previously learned material or making simple interpretations. Abilities include translating material to new forms, explaining and summarizing material, and

estimating future trends. Comprehension-level objectives can be expressed with such verbs as: translate, convert, generalize, paraphrase, rewrite, summarize, differentiate, defend, infer, and explain. Comprehension-level examples include:

After reading a short story, the student will summarize the major plot.

After studying the Civil War, the student will explain the conditions in the South and North that led to the war.

3. **Application** entails the use of learned information in new and concrete situations. It may involve the application of rules, general ideas, concepts, laws, principles, and theories. Application-level objectives can be expressed with such verbs as: use, operate, produce, change, solve, show, compute, and prepare. Application-level examples include:

Using two different algorithmic forms, the student will solve two-digit addition problems.

The student will prepare a graph showing the United States's exports for the last 10 years.

4. **Analysis** entails breaking down material into its component parts so it can be better understood. It may involve identification of components, analysis of relationships between parts, and recognition of organizational principles and structures. Analysis-level objectives can be expressed with such verbs as: discriminate, select, distinguish, separate, subdivide, identify, and break down. Analysis-level examples include:

Given a sentence, the student will identify the major parts of speech.

The student will break down a story plot into various subplots.

5. **Creation** entails combining components to form a new whole or to produce an evaluation based on specified criteria. It may involve the creation of a unique composition, communication, plan, proposal, or scheme for classifying information. The unique creation may require that a judgment regarding the value of material be made based on an internal or external criteria. Creation-level objectives can be expressed with such verbs as: design, plan, compile, compose, organize, appraise, compare, justify, conclude, criticize, explain, and interpret. Creation-level examples include:

The student will compose an original story from an unusual situation.

Given the materials, the student will design a hat.

Levels of Affective Learning

Learning intent in the affective domain is organized according to the degree of internalization. That is, it is organized according to the degree to which an attitude, feeling, value, or emotion has become part of the individual. As adapted from the work of Krathwohl (1964), four levels of learning are included in the affective taxonomy.

1. **Receiving** involves being aware of and being willing to *freely* attend to a stimulus (listen and look). Receiving-level objectives can be expressed with such verbs as: follow, select, rely, choose, point to, ask, hold, give, and locate. Receiving-level examples include:

The student will listen for respect words in stories read aloud in class.

When asked, the student will hold various science animals.

2. **Responding** involves active participation. It involves not only *freely* attending to a stimulus but also *voluntarily* reacting to it in some way. It requires physical, active behavior. Responding-level objectives can be expressed with verbs such as: read, conform, help, answer, practice, present, report, greet, tell, and perform. Responding-level examples include:

The student will volunteer to help with a class mathematics project.

The student will report that poetry is enjoyable to read.

3. **Valuing** refers to voluntarily giving worth to an object, phenomenon, or stimulus. Behaviors at this level reflect a belief, appreciation, or attitude. Valuing-level objectives can be expressed with such verbs as: initiate, ask, invite, share, join, follow, propose, read, study, and work. Valuing-level examples include:

When given a center choice, the student will ask to go to the science learning center.

The student will join at least one discussion of a school-related subject.

4. **Commitment** involves building an internally consistent value system and *freely* living by it. A set of criteria is established

and applied in choice making. Commitment-level objectives can be expressed with such verbs as: adhere, defend, alter, integrate, relate, synthesize, act, listen, serve, influence, use, and verify. Commitment-level examples include:

The student will defend the importance of at least one governmental social policy.

The student will freely alter a judgment in light of new evidence.

Levels of Psychomotor Learning

Learning intent in the psychomotor domain ranges from acquiring the basic rudiments of a motor skill to the perfection of a complex skill. In this text three levels of learning are included in the psychomotor taxonomy.

1. **Imitation** refers to the ability to carry out the basic rudiments of a skill when given directions and under supervision. At this level the total act is not performed with skill, nor is timing and coordination refined. Imitation-level objectives can be expressed with verbs such as: construct, dismantle, drill, change, clean, manipulate, follow, and use. Imitation-level examples include:

Given written instruction, the student will construct at least five geometric models.

The student will follow basic instructions for making a simple table.

2. **Manipulation** refers to the ability to perform a skill independently. The entire skill can be performed in sequence. Conscious effort is no longer needed to perform the skill, but complete accuracy has not been achieved. Manipulation-level objectives can be expressed with verbs such as: connect, create, fasten, make, sketch, weigh, wrap, and manipulate. Manipulation-level examples include:

Given several different objects, the student will weigh each.

Given an oral description of an object, the student will sketch it.

3. **Precision** refers to the ability to perform an act accurately, efficiently, and harmoniously. Complete coordination of the skill has been acquired. The skill has been internalized to the extent that it can be performed unconsciously. Precision-level objectives can be expressed by such terms as: focus, align, adjust, calibrate, construct, manipulate, and build. Precision-level examples include:

The student will accurately adjust a microscope.

Given the materials, the student will construct a usable chair.

This concludes our formal discussion of the three domains of learning. Table 3.4 gives an overview of the taxonomies. Remember that the taxonomies can be a valuable tool for upgrading your writing of objectives. However, do not become a slave to the taxonomies. Base your objectives on the needs of the class. Use the taxonomies only as a guide and strive to incorporate the higher levels of each taxonomy in your learning experiences.

TABLE 3.4   The Three Educational Domains with Levels of Learning and Definitions.

DOMAIN OR LEVEL	DEFINITION
Cognitive Domain	
1. Knowledge	Recall of factual information
2. Comprehension	Lowest level of understanding; giving evidence of understanding and the ability to make use of information
3. Application	Use of abstractions or principles to solve problems.
4. Analysis	Distinguishing and comprehending interrelationships
5. Creation	Combining components to form a new whole
Affective Domain	
1. Receiving	Freely attending to stimuli
2. Responding	Voluntarily reacting to stimuli
3. Valuing	Forming an attitude toward a stimulus
4. Characterization	Behaving consistently with an internally developed, stable value system
Psychomotor Domain	
1. Imitation	Carry out basic skill with directions and under supervision
2. Manipulation	Perform a skill independently
3. Precision	Perform a skill accurately

Now focus your attention for a few minutes on Task 3.5, which will check your understanding of the three taxonomies.

TASK 3.5   Objective Taxonomies

Answer the following questions. Check your responses with those given at the end of the chapter.

1. List and define the three major domains for classifying objectives.

   a. _____

   _____

   b. _____

   _____

   c. _____

   _____

2. Most educators find it easier to write objectives for the affective domain than the cognitive domain.   (True/False)

3. You, as a teacher, should be proficient at writing objectives at all the specific taxonomy levels of the three domains of learning. (True/False)

4. The creation of a unique entity from basic components would fall into one of the higher levels of cognitive learning.   (True/False)

5. The ability to perform a skill accurately would indicate only lower-level psychomotor learning.   (True/False)

COMMUNICATION OF OBJECTIVES

As stated at the beginning of this chapter, communicating objectives to students is absolutely necessary if you are to get maximum value from them. The communication can be accomplished through the use of either verbal or written statements or through a combination of both.

With younger students or those who have limited reading abilities, it is usually wise to communicate your objectives verbally. This is usually accomplished during the introductory phase of your lesson by translating the written objective(s) into appropriate verbal statements which communicate your intent. Care should be taken, however, that the translated material is in a form that is understandable. This translation process is discussed in greater detail in Chapter 4.

With older students multiple objectives are usually shared at the beginning of a unit of study and are presented in written form. One useful format for presenting multiple unit objectives is to list each individual objective with only the performance verb and product. For example:

After completing the unit, you should be able to:

1. Identify (write) percents illustrated with 100-part graph paper, with pie shapes, and with various rectangular shapes.
2. Illustrate (shade) numerical percents with 100-part graph paper, with pie shapes, and with various rectangular shapes.
3. Rewrite common fractions and decimal fractions as percents.
4. Rewrite percents as common fractions and decimal fractions.
5. Work simple percent problems.

Another useful format for stating multiple instructional objectives is to use an introductory statement to communicate common conditions and the criterion level. The remainder of each individual objective is then listed with the performance verb, the product, and specific conditions. For example:

After completing the unit Learning about Sentences you should be able to perform the following objectives with seventy percent proficiency on the unit exam:

1. Define the terms *simple subject* and *simple predicate.*
2. Identify (underline) the simple subject and simple predicate in a given sentence.
3. Define a simple and a compound sentence.
4. Identify (check) simple and compound sentences.
5. Define the terms *compound subject* and *compound predicate.*
6. Identify (underline) the compound subject and compound predicate in a given sentence.
7. Diagram the simple subject and simple predicate in a given sentence.
8. Diagram the compound subject and compound predicate in a given sentence.

The exact format used to communicate your objectives to students is not critical. The important thing is that you communicate precise information regarding your instructional intent. In most cases using the more informal "you" in your objective introductory phrase rather than the formal "the student" is preferable when the objectives are to be read by the students. The "you" will personalize your objectives.

SUMMARY

Stating objectives is one of the most crucial components of the planning process. They specify teaching intent, that is, what your students should be able to do following instruction. They tell you and the students where you are going. Therefore, objectives should be stated in terms of terminal student behaviors that are overt and observable.

Specification of learning intent varies from extremely broad educational goals to very narrow, specific objectives. The three levels of learning intent, in order of specificity, are educational goals, informational objectives, and instructional objectives. The more specific objectives should be subordinate to major educational goals. The behaviors called for by educational goals are covert, whereas the behaviors called for by informational and instructional objectives are overt. In addition educational goals and objectives may be written for the cognitive, affective, or psychomotor domains of learning.

Well-stated instructional objectives consist of four components: the performance, the product, the conditions, and the criterion. Informational objectives, on the other hand, specify only the performance and the product; the conditions and criterion are usually not specified. In most cases informational objectives suffice for communicating learning intent.

Your objectives should always be communicated to students. This communication can be in either verbal or written form. However, the communication of objectives should not have as an intent to limit learning only to those areas specified in the objectives. Objectives are intended only to provide a minimum level of learning. Other incidental learning should be expected and encouraged as students progress through the objectives.

TASK 3.1   Identifying Verbs

1. O   2. O   3. O   4. C   5. O   6. C   7. O   8. C   9. C

TASK 3.2   Identifying the Components of Well-Stated Objectives

1. Given a set of pictures, the student will be able to place the [pictures in proper sequence] with no more than one error.

2. Given the necessary materials and the dimensions, the student will be able to (construct) [a polygon] with all dimensions being within 5 percent.

3. The student will be able to (identify (select letter)) on a multiple-choice test [the subplots of the poems read in class] with 100 percent accuracy.

4. After completing a series of Spanish language tapes, the student will be able to (orally recite) a given [Spanish dialogue] with no errors in pronunciation.

5. The student will be able to (write) a [300-word essay] on a given social studies topic with no sentence fragments and no more than two errors in grammar.

TASK 3.3   Objective Concepts

1. a. Assists in determining appropriate teaching approach
   b. Sets framework for evaluation
   c. Assists in communicating learning intent to students

2. *False*   One should always share objectives with students. It takes the guessing out of learning.

3. a. Educational goals
   b. Informational objectives
   c. Instructional objectives

4. a. *The performance*   The action to be carried out by the students
   b. *The product*   The end results of the performance
   c. *The conditions*   The conditions under which the performance will occur
   d. *The criterion*   The acceptable level of performance

5. *False*   Informational objectives usually contain only the performance and the product.

TASK 3.4   Identifying the Domain of Objectives

1. P   2. C   3. P   4. A   5. C   6. P   7. A   8. C   9. A   10. C

TASK 3.5   Objective Taxonomies

1. a. *Cognitive domain*   This area is concerned with imparting knowledge and with the thinking process.

    b. *Affective domain*   This area is concerned with emotional development.

    c. *Psychomotor domain*   This area is concerned with the development of physical skills.

2. *False*   Most educators find affective domain objectives the most difficult to write.

3. *True*   You should be able to write objectives at all taxonomic levels. However, you should write objectives for the intended learning and not write objectives for the specific level because it is the thing to do.

4. *True*   It would involve thinking at the creation level of the cognitive domain.

5. *False*   Accurate performance would indicate higher level psychomotor learning had taken place. In fact accurate performance indicates psychomotor learning at the precision level.

ACTIVITIES

1. *Analysis of textbook objectives*   Review the teacher's edition of a textbook that lists the unit or chapter objectives for a topic from your area of specialization. Address the following questions in your review.

    a. Are educational goals presented? informational objectives? instructional objectives?

    b. Are objectives written for all three domains of learning?

    c. Are the objectives written at different levels within each of the learning domains?

2. *Writing goals and objectives*   Write an educational goal for an area in your specialization. Now write informational and instructional objectives that tell what students should do to show that the goal has been accomplished.

3. *Writing cognitive, psychomotor, and affective domain objectives* Write 10 cognitive and psychomotor domain objectives for the class of your choice. Make the objectives at various levels of sophistication. Now write five affective domain objectives at various levels for the same class. Submit the objectives to your instructor for analysis.

REFERENCES

Beane, J. A., Toepfer, C. F., Jr., Alessi, S. J., Jr. (1986). *Curriculum Planning and Development.* Boston: Allyn and Bacon.

Blenkin, G. M., and Kelly, A. V. (1981). *The Primary Curriculum.* New York: Harper and Row.

Bloom, B. S. (Ed.), Engelhart, M. D., Furst, E. J., Hill, W. H., and Krathwohl, D. R. (1956). *Taxonomy of Educational Objectives, Handbook I: Cognitive Domain.* New York: David McKay.

Davies, G. M. (1976). *Objectives in Curriculum Design.* New York: McGraw Hill.

Gronlund, N. E. (1970). *Stating Behavioral Objectives for Classroom Instruction.* New York: Macmillan.

Kibler, R. J., Barker, L. L., and Miles, D. T. (1970). *Behavioral Objectives and Instruction.* Boston: Allyn and Bacon.

Krathwohl, D. R., Bloom, B. S., and Masai, B. B. (1964). *Taxonomy of Educational Objectives, Handbook II: Affective Domain.* New York: David McKay.

Kryspin, W. J., and Feldhusen, J. F. (1974). *Writing Behavioral Objectives.* Minneapolis, Minn.: Burgess.

Mager, R. F. (1984). *Preparing Instructional Objectives,* 2d ed. Belmont, Calif.: David S. Lake.

Planning the Presentation

After completing your study of Chapter 4, you should be able to:

1. Describe the four levels of planning
2. Explain the importance of daily lesson planning in the learning process
3. Identify and describe the three key components of a daily plan
4. Operationally define set induction
5. Explain the three purposes of a strong set induction
6. Operationally define instructional strategy and name the two areas that make up the instructional strategy
7. Describe the four variables that should be considered in the selection of an appropriate instructional strategy
8. Explain the importance of lesson closure to effective teaching
9. Write appropriate set inductions and closures for selected topics

FIGURE 4.1 Levels of Planning.

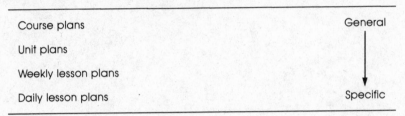

The presentations of effective teachers usually appear so spontaneous that no planning is apparent. However, very probably these teachers have indeed—formally or informally—carefully planned each daily lesson. They have likely mastered the lesson content and the related teaching skills so well that they are poised, secure, and automatic in their delivery.

Even experienced teachers spend time replanning the presentation of lessons that they have taught several times. In this way they continue to improve their presentations and avoid becoming stale and routine. However, no amount of planning can ensure success. It is the way presentations are delivered that really counts.

LEVELS OF PLANNING

As shown in Figure 4.1, teachers engage in various levels of planning. Course and unit planning has much greater scope than weekly and daily planning. Your course and unit plans give the more specific daily plans their direction and determine in a general way what the impact of the entire curriculum will be.

Course and Unit Planning

The most general type of planning you will do as a classroom teacher is course planning. In this general long-range plan, you lay out your instruction for the year for each subject. That is, you outline and sequence the units of study for the year and make unit time allotments, as in the following example.

Unit 1   The Birth of a Nation   (*3 weeks*)

        Chapter 1   The Immigrant Experience

        Chapter 2   The Colonial Experience

        Chapter 3   Of War and Revolution

Unit 2   The Constitution   (*3 weeks*)
Chapter   4   Framing the Constitution
Chapter   5   The Constitution of the United States
Chapter   6   The New Nation

Unit 3   The New Nation   (*4 weeks*)
Chapter   7   Crises of the New Nation
Chapter   9   American Life and Letters
Chapter 10   The Peculiar Institution

Unit 4   The Divided Nation   (*4 weeks*)
Chapter 11   Westward Expansion
Chapter 12   Sectional Conflict and the Gathering Storm
Chapter 13   The Civil War
Chapter 14   The War's Aftermath

Unit 5   The Indivisible Nation   (*6 weeks*)
Chapter 15   Farm, Forge, and Factory
Chapter 17   Imperial America
Chapter 18   The United States and World War I
Chapter 19   The Tired Twenties

Unit 6   This Urban Nation   (*4 weeks*)
Chapter 20   The City and Its People
Chapter 21   The Shame of the Cities
Chapter 22   The Cry for Reform
Chapter 23   The Culture of City Life

Unit 7   The Great Depression   (*2 weeks*)
Chapter 24   The Great Depression and the New Deal

Unit 8   The Nation Comes of Age   (*4 weeks*)
Chapter 25   War Clouds Again
Chapter 26   The United States in World War II
Chapter 27   Uncertain Peace
Chapter 28   Postwar Politics and Problems

Unit 9   A New Road for America   (*4 weeks*)
Chapter 29   The New Frontier at Home and Abroad
Chapter 30   Toward the Great Society
Chapter 32   The Worst or the Best of Times?

The course plan should be flexible so changes can be made during the year as the need arises. As you select chapters to be assigned, recognize that not all chapters need to be covered, the text sequence is not always the best for every class, and all chapters are not of equal importance. Also make time allotments based upon your intended methods and procedures and on the importance of the topic.

One of the chief values of course planning is that it permits you to gather more and better media and instructional materials (films, special equipment, computer programs, special books, etc.) by the time they are needed. In fact some school districts even require that all special materials be requested at the beginning of the year. In such districts course planning is essential.

Courses, as listed above, are usually divided into units of study that represent discrete segments of the year's work in a given subject. Each unit is organized around a specific topic, theme, or major concept. Thus, a unit is a series of many intended learning activities and experiences unified around the topic, theme, or major concept. More specifically, a well-constructed unit should include the following sections:

1. *A topic.* Presumably the topic will be suggested by the course outline, a textbook, or a curriculum guide.

2. *Goals and objectives.* This is a listing of your learning intent in broad and specific terms.

3. *Content outline.* An outline of the content to be covered with as much detail as you feel is needed. This outline should help clarify the subject and help you with the organization.

4. *Learning activities.* These are the activities (teacher and student) that will lead to the desired learning. They should include introductory, developmental, and culminating activities. The activities should be arranged into a series of daily lessons.

5. *Resources and materials.* This includes a listing of materials to be selected and prepared for the unit.

6. *Evaluation.* An outline of your evaluation procedure. It could include projects, homework, or tests. Tests and evaluative exercises should be planned and prepared prior to instruction.

The units can vary greatly in scope and duration, depending on the grade level and subject. Generally they range in duration from a week to six weeks. Other examples of typical units are community helpers in kindergarten, transportation in the second grade, the library in the sixth grade, astronomy in the eighth grade, and photosynthesis in high school biology.

Weekly and Daily Lesson Plans

Many schools ask that teachers submit weekly lesson plans so that, in the event they become ill, a substitute teacher would have some idea of what was to be covered that day. Weekly lesson plans vary greatly in detail depending on the school. Essentially they are watered-down copies of the week's daily lesson plans written on special forms provided by the school.

The most specific type of plan is a daily lesson plan, which is simply the class activities for a single day. Thus, unit planning does not eliminate daily planning. However, since the objectives, general activities, experiences, and necessary materials have been specified in the well-done unit plan, the daily lesson plan flows naturally out of the unit plan. It should include the following sections:

1. *Objectives.*   The specific learning intent for the day selected from the unit plan

2. *Introduction.*   An activity to be used to begin the lesson

3. *Content.*   A brief outline of the content to be covered in the lesson

4. *Methods and procedure.*   A listing of the developmental activities

5. *Closure.*   The lesson wrap-up activity

6. *Resources and materials.*   A listing of instructional materials needed for the lesson

7. *Assignment.*   The in-class or homework assignment to be completed for the next class period

Instructional Materials

Surveying available media and preparing materials for instruction are essential to effective planning. Textbooks, audiovisual materials, supplementary reading materials, and supplies and equipment for group and individual projects should be procured and coordinated with your lesson. Taking the time to familiarize yourself with what is available in the district will be time well spent. You should review printed materials, preview films, listen to records, and learn to use the latest technology.

Students with Special Needs

Some of your students will be academically bright while others are slow; some will be socially skillful while others are inept. You must learn to modify your instruction to fit the individual needs and interests of the students. The modifications will include such things as developing special dittos to help teach difficult concepts, modifying assigned work, developing special study guides, changing grouping patterns to fit special needs, or obtaining and using special equipment with the physically handicapped or gifted.

Teachers with mainstreamed or special students must learn to give differentiated assignments. You can do this by varying the length or difficulty of assignments. For example in a mathematics class, you might assign 5 problems to your slow students, 10 problems to the average students, and 10 more difficult problems to the better students. Similarly you might require only half as much writing from children who experience motor difficulties.

Another approach is to vary the type of work students do. Some students should be allowed to complete and submit their written assignments on a word processor. Creative students may occasionally be allowed to create something instead of writing a report. Students might sometimes be allowed to assist each other.

Some general planning guidelines for working with students who have special needs include:

1. Learning about the nature of the exceptional student's difference and how that difference might affect the learning process

2. Determining if help is available from a special education or resource expert

3. Determining the exceptional student's equipment needs to allow him or her to function at an optimum level

4. Considering how to adapt the curriculum and your teaching strategies to better serve the needs of the exceptional student

5. Considering how to individualize the curriculum as much as possible.

6. Providing for the removal of barriers, both physical and psychological, that inhibit the exceptional student's full functioning.

Having identified and briefly looked at the four levels of planning, let us now look at daily lesson planning in more detail. As might be expected, teachers vary widely in their approach to daily planning. Some develop detailed daily plans, whereas others merely write out a few notes as reminders. Regardless of the amount of detail or general format, your daily plan should consist of three key ingredients: the set induction (cognitive set), the lesson itself (strategy and procedure), and the lesson closure.

SET INDUCTION

Set induction is what you do at the outset of a lesson, that is, what you do to get students' undivided attention, to arouse their interest, and to establish a conceptual framework for the information to follow.

Student Attention

Until your students are prepared to listen (have a cognitive set), it is usually unwise to begin a lesson. Your opening remarks, frequently related to the homework assignment or some recent lesson, will have to be repeated if you have not gained their attention. On special days (holidays, Big Game days, stormy days, etc.), you will find it particularly difficult to get and maintain their attention. On such days you must take special care with the introduction.

Teachers can use a variety of techniques to gain student attention. One of the most frequently used and most effective techniques is to do nothing. Simply stand silently facing the class. Soon the entire class will be drawn to the silence. The lack of customary teacher talk arouses students' interest and attention. This technique is especially effective when you have a small group within the class that is inattentive. Silence and an intense stare in the group's direction will soon get their undivided attention.

Another attention-getting technique is to begin speaking in a very low tone and gradually raise your voice to normal volume when the class is quiet and attentive. If used often, this technique can even become a signal to be quiet and pay attention. In a sense you have conditioned the class to become attentive on the signal.

Gestures and teacher movement can also be effective attention getters. Students, like most people, are naturally drawn to any type of movement. For example, waving your hand, practicing your golf swing, or walking toward noisy students can direct attention to yourself. Experimenting with various movements will determine which ones are most effective with a particular class. Classes will differ based on such factors as course content, socioeconomic level, family background, motivation, grade level, and class size.

To summarize, silence, voice control, and movement can all be used effectively to gain student attention at the onset of a lesson. However, the establishment of cognitive set is not their only use as you will see in later chapters.

Student Interest and Involvement

The second purpose of the set induction is to establish student interest and involvement in the forthcoming lesson. Thus, your introduction should act as a lesson motivator. It should, as much as possible, create an atmosphere of, "Tell me more; this sounds interesting." Motivation can be quite difficult at times, for no matter what teaching strategies you employ, some topics are of little interest to students. However, regardless of the topic, you can always try to be creative.

One method of developing student interest is to begin the lesson by relating it to a topic of vital interest to the class. The topic itself need not even be closely related to the lesson. For example interest in music can lead into a study of sound. School elections can serve as a lead to the United States political system. Or a discussion of home pets can be used to introduce a unit on animals. This technique is an art that needs to be practiced and refined. Listen to the conversations of your students for topics that you can use to start your lessons. A simple remark related to the topic will usually get the discussion started.

Suspense can also create interest and involvement. Begin the class with an interesting demonstration or a discrepant event. For example demonstrate a volcano in earth science, show an airplane in flight when introducing a story on air travel in reading, or mix paints to form various paint colors in art. Make the demonstration or discrepant event as novel or surprising as possible. Even better, involve students in the introductory demonstration or in showing the event.

Models, diagrams, or pictures situated in visible spots are effective in capturing attention and interest. You might begin the lesson by soliciting student comments. For example you might ask the class to guess the model's function or what the diagram or picture represents.

Questions and hypothetical cases are also effective in establishing sets. To be effective, however, they must stimulate student curiosity or interest. For example questions such as, "What would happen if . . ?" are excellent for gaining interest. When the right conditions are attached, hypothetical cases that deal with the unknown or the presentation of a puzzling situation are often successful. For example ask what effect no school would have on their life, show an ice cube sinking in a clear liquid that looks like water, or show a piece of wood that will not burn. However, if you decide to create sets by using questions or hypothetical cases, make sure they are strong. Too often teachers use questions or cases that are ineffective and, consequently, weaken the future success of this technique.

Establishing a Framework

Students learn more when they know what to expect from a lesson. Thus to maximize learning your introductory remarks should provide students with what Ausubel (1963) calls an **advance organizer;** that is, your opening remarks should give students a "what to look for" frame of reference. In a sense the concept of advance organizer is related closely to the establishment of student interest but is usually more specific in nature.

Advance organizers can be generalizations, definitions, or analogies (Orlich et al., 1980). For example a science teacher might start a lesson on animal life with a generalization about the major characteristics of life. A second grade teacher might start a math lesson with definitions of the new vocabulary words. Or a social studies teacher might start a lesson on war by relating it to a tennis match. No matter what form it takes, the purpose of an advance organizer is either to give students the background information they need to make sense of the upcoming lesson or to help them remember and apply old information to the lesson. Thus, the organizer acts as a kind of conceptual bridge between the new and old information.

Many teachers use a verbal statement of the lesson objective(s) as the advance organizer. However, in using this technique you must take care to translate the written objective(s) into a form that is both understandable and interesting to students. An example of this technique is:

Objective   The students will be able to correctly calculate the impact speed of a dropped object.

Translation [Teacher holds an object overhead.]: When I drop this object, watch it closely. [Teacher drops object.] There was a continuous increase in the object's speed as it fell. But, it fell so fast that the increase was impossible to detect. What was its speed upon impact? [Silence.] That's what we're going to find out today.

To summarize, you must set the stage for the learning process. If you fail to arouse student attention and interest, the remainder of the lesson is often wasted. In addition a framework for the lesson must also be established in order to maximize learning. Therefore, in most cases your introductory remarks (set) should consist of two parts: the attention getter/motivator and the advance organizer.

Let us now assess your understanding of various set induction techniques. Take a few minutes to complete Task 4.1.

TASK 4.1   Identifying Set Induction Techniques

For each statement given, indicate whether the technique would be effective for gaining student attention and interest (A) or for providing students with a framework for the lesson (F). If you feel the example would be ineffective as a set induction technique, leave it blank. Check your responses with those given at the end of the chapter.

_____   1.   "Today we're going to learn to subtract decimal fractions. The procedure is very much like the procedure we learned for subtracting common fractions."

_____   2.   "John, come up and show us with this model how you think our solar system works."

_____   3.   "Let's get to work on today's lesson."

_____   4.   "Have any of you noticed the strange diagram on the board? What do you suppose it is?"

_____   5.   "Let's go over our new vocabulary words and their meaning before we read the story."

THE LESSON

A lesson consists of the content to be taught as well as the instructional strategy employed in teaching that content. This section of your plan should contain, in the order of implementation, a listing of the topics, skills, and activities that you want to cover during the instructional period. The details included in this section will vary between individuals. However, the information should be detailed enough to serve as a memory jogger. Thus, you should include all the information needed to remind you of your plan of action. Perhaps a few brief notes will suffice. Perhaps a detailed description of content, activities, and questions will be needed. The details are entirely up to you. After all you will be the one using the plan.

Instructional strategy consists of two components: the methodology and the procedure. The methodology "sets the tone" of the lesson. It should act as the student "motivator." Commonly used methods include: the inquiry approach, the discovery approach, the discussion method, a demonstration, role playing, and the lecture. The method should be selected and planned so that it captures and holds the attention of the students and involves them as much as possible in the learning situation. The procedure differs in that it is the "outline" for implementing the lesson. It provides the sequence of steps that has been designed to lead the students to to the acquisition of the objectives. For example you may decide on the following sequence for a lesson on Japanese history:

1. Present short introductory lecture on the history of Japan
2. Show a film on Japan
3. Conduct summary discussion on film content
4. Conduct question and answer session on major points covered in the lecture and in the film

As you see, the procedure consists of the sequenced teacher and student activities used to carry out the lesson.

Your instructional strategy is the actual presentation of the lesson content, that is, how you will give students the information. This requires that you choose from a wide variety of methods and learning experiences what you feel will best lead to the desired learning.

Orlich and associates (1980) identify four variables that affect the selection of the appropriate instructional strategy for a particular lesson. These variables include the content and objectives of the lesson, teacher characteristics, learner characteristics, and the learning environment.

Every lesson must have a purpose. What is yours? Are you trying to teach in the cognitive, affective, or psychomotor domains? Obviously your selection of methodology and experiences will be related to the teaching domain. In addition the methodology should be related to such factors as the goals, specific learning objectives, and content. For example if you are trying to teach problem solving or a psychomotor skill, the lecture method is not a desirable approach.

Every teacher has a unique set of personal experiences, background knowledge, teaching skills, and personality traits that make them more comfortable and effective with certain methodologies than others. Obviously most teachers select the methods that have proven most successful in the past. Because everyone is inclined to select the methodology that makes them feel most comfortable, it is easy to get into a teaching rut. Be prepared to experiment with different methods. You cannot become familiar and comfortable with methods you have not used. Remember that you, too, are a learner.

The particular methodology selected must also match the maturity level and experiences of your students. You would not use the lecture method with very young students or with those who have trouble paying attention to verbal messages. Students, like teachers, feel comfortable and learn better when the method fits their abilities, needs, and interests. Always keep in mind that when the method is mismatched with your students, learning will not take place at the maximum level. Thus, effective teachers select the best possible method for a particular class.

Obviously the selected method may not always be the best one for every student in the class, but it should be the best fit for the class as a whole. To truly fit the abilities, needs, and interests of every student in a class, you must individualize the instruction. However, individualizing instruction does not mean that you should rely solely on individual seatwork. You should always use direct instruction (active teacher-centered instruction) to some extent even when individualizing. After all you, the teacher, are still responsible for organizing the content and directing the learning process. This point cannot be overemphasized.

Finally the environment and related factors should be taken into account when selecting your methodology. Such factors as space available, time of day, and weather can influence a lesson and should be considered in selecting the methodology. For example one would not select a method that required a high level of concentration and little activity late in the school day or on days when there has been a drastic weather change. Also if you have little space and a large class, the discovery approach might not be appropriate.

No matter how much detail you include in your written lesson plan or what instructional strategy you employ, the lesson must be well structured to be successful. The structure should include techniques that will keep students interested and motivated. Henson (1981) suggests several techniques:

1. Actively involve students in the lesson through meaningful activities.

2. Make the content as relevant as possible.

3. Keep the instructional atmosphere as informal as possible.

4. Be enthusiastic about the material you are teaching.

5. Keep students challenged through the use of problems, inconsistencies, and contradictions throughout the lesson.

6. Share your goals and procedures with students so they know where they are going and how they are going to get there.

7. Use the ideas and opinions expressed by students so they feel you value their input.

Attention to these suggestions and to those factors that should be considered in selecting an instructional strategy will lead to more effective instruction. The result should then be enhanced learning on the part of your students.

CLOSURE

Once your lesson has been concluded, the main points and concepts must be pulled together so they are organized and integrated within the students' existing cognitive structure. This is accomplished in your lesson closure.

Closure should be more than a quick review of the points covered in the lesson. It should enable students to organize the new material in relation to itself and to other lessons. Closure is as vital to the teaching-learning process as is set induction and the lesson itself.

Sometimes you may want to achieve closure during the course of a particular lesson. Shostak (1982) suggests that closure is appropriate in the following situations:

1. To end a long unit of study

2. To consolidate the learning of a new concept

3. To close a group discussion

4. To follow up a film, record, play, or T.V. program

5. To summarize experiences of a field trip

6. To summarize the presentation of a guest speaker

7. To end a science experiment

These situations represent only a few activities that might call for closure. An important part of instruction is being able to judge when closure is needed.

Allen et al. (1969) suggest five different ways that closure can be accomplished. First, you can organize your content around a central theme, generalization, or model. Either the teacher or the students can then relate the material covered back to the organizing theme, generalization, or model. Examples include such statements as ''The characteristics of this play make it an excellent example of a tragedy,'' or ''These proofs support our original generalization that a negative number times a negative number result in a positive number,'' or ''This form of government fits our model of a democracy.''

Second, you can achieve closure through the use of cueing. This can take the form of an outline on the chalkboard, which helps students organize the material by outlining the major points covered, or you can simply use cueing statements such as "The main parts are as follows . . ." or "There are three important points to remember. First, . . ." Cueing can be effectively used at any point in a lesson and is often used at several points when new concepts are being developed.

Third, you can draw attention to the completion of the lesson through the use of summary questions. Questions such as "What were the four major points covered in today's lesson?" or "Mike, can you summarize today's lesson?" or "Can you draw any conclusions from our discussion?" can be used effectively to close a lesson.

Fourth, connecting new and previously learned material helps students achieve closure. For example structured statements, such as "Let's relate this to yesterday's study of addition," or "This form of government is similar to the other forms of government we have studied," or "Can we relate this example to examples we have studied in the past?"

Finally, a commonly used and effective way to achieve closure is to let students demonstrate or apply what they have learned. If the new concept or skill cannot be demonstrated or applied, it has not been learned. Examples of this technique include such teacher questions or statements as "Can you give me other examples of nouns and pronouns?" or "Let's diagram the two sentences at the top of page 56 like we did these examples," or "Let's do the oral exercises in the book together." Demonstrating or applying the new information at the conclusion of the lesson has the added advantage of providing immediate feedback to the students. Many teachers have students do worksheets or in-class assignments to achieve closure by application and to provide immediate feedback to the students.

It is important that every student in your class achieve closure on a lesson. Just because one student demonstrates closure does not necessarily mean that all have achieved it.

Task 4.2 further refines your skill at lesson closure. Complete it before you continue.

TASK 4.2   Identifying Appropriate Lesson Closures

For each example indicate whether the teacher used a closure technique that was appropriate (A) or not appropriate (NA) Check your responses with those given at the end of the chapter.

_____ 1. As the bell rings the teacher gives the students an assignment that requires application of the lesson content.

_____ 2. "Let's now review the major concepts we have studied in today's lesson."

_____ 3. With 10 minutes left in the period, the teacher has the students work on the homework assignment so she can assist them as needed.

_____ 4. "Are there any questions on how to write a declarative sentence?"

_____ 5. "John, can you tell us how the material we covered today is similar to the material we covered in the lesson we had last week?"

This completes our formal discussion of techniques for planning your daily lessons. Task 4.3 checks your understanding of the concepts presented in this chapter.

TASK 4.3 Presentation Concepts

Answer the following questions. Check your responses with those given at the end of the chapter.

1. List and describe four levels of teacher planning.

a. _____

_____

b. _____

_____

c. _____

_____

d. _____

_____

2. Name and describe the three ingredients of a well-planned presentation.

a. _____

_____

b. _____

_____

c. _____
_____

3. Describe the three purposes of a set induction.

a. _____
_____

b. _____
_____

c. _____
_____

4. The methodology to be used in a lesson consists of the actual activities, in sequential order, that will be conducted in a lesson presentation.   (True/False)

5. Name the four variables that affect the instructional strategy you
choose to employ in a lesson.

a. _____
_____

b. _____
_____

c. _____
_____

d. _____
_____

6. Describe five ways to achieve closure in a lesson.

a. _____
_____

b. _____
_____

c. _____
_____

d. _____
_____

e. _____
_____

SUMMARY

Planning is essential to effective teaching. Therefore, teachers must plan and plan well. Courses must be planned, units must be developed, and weekly plans must be written. Lastly and most important, daily lesson plans must be developed and implemented.

Planning your daily lesson presentation should be viewed as a tool for effective teaching. If your daily lessons are not leading to better learning, you should review and revise your techniques. Perhaps you need to pay more attention to your opening or your lesson activities or your closing.

A strong beginning (set induction) is crucial for any activity or lesson. It establishes the tone and sets a conceptual framework for the coming activities. It should be planned so that the immediate attention of every student is captured. If you jump into a lesson before a cognitive set is established, your students may miss the important beginning of your lesson.

The lesson instructional strategy consists of your methodology and procedure. The strategy forms the heart of your lesson and should be chosen with care. Take into account your objectives, your abilities, the intended learners, and the environment. Always keep in mind that the prime purpose of your strategy is to bring about the acquisition of the intended learning. One maxim to keep in mind in selecting a strategy is that "students must participate." They should respond in some manner or at the least be mentally alert.

Your lesson should also have a definite ending. This can be done with a summary, a recapitulation of what was covered, a series of open-ended questions, or student application of the covered concepts. This ending should be planned and accomplished before the closing bell rings.

Attention to the three components of a daily lesson will lead to stronger lessons. In fact a good rule to remember is to spend adequate time on each of these components. The results will be well worth the effort.

Answer Keys

TASK 4.1   Identifying Set Induction Techniques

1. F A framework is established for the subtraction of decimal fractions.
2. A Student attention and interest should be gained.
3. (blank)
4. A Diagram should gain student attention.
5. F A framework is established through the use of an advance organizer.

TASK 4.2   Identifying Appropriate Lesson Closures

1. *NA*

2. *A*   Major concepts reviewed

3. *A*   In-class application and feedback provided

4. *NA*

5. *A*   Material related to previous learning

TASK 4.3   Presentation Concepts

1. a. *Course planning*   Course planning is long-range planning in which instruction for the year is layed out.

   b. *Unit planning*   A unit plan is a segment of the year's work organized around a specific topic, theme, or a major concept.

   c. *Weekly planning*   A weekly plan is a collection of daily plans for the week.

   d. *Daily lesson planning*   A daily lesson plan is the presentation for a single day.

2. a. *Set induction*   The set is what you do at the outset of a lesson to get student attention, to trigger their interest, and to establish a conceptual framework.

   b. *Lesson*   The content to be taught and the instructional strategy to be used to teach it.

   c. *Closure*   This is the summing up of the lesson. The new material is tied together and tied to previous learning.

3. a. To get student attention

   b. To get students interested and involved

   c. To establish a framework for the content to be taught

4. *False*   The actual activities to be used in a lesson presentation is the procedure.

5. a. The content and objectives of the lesson

   b. The personality and characteristics of the teacher

   c. The characteristics of the learner

   d. The environment

6. Responses may vary considerably. However, five possible closure techniques are:

   a. Relate material to central theme, generalization, or model.

   b. Outline major points on the overhead projector or chalkboard.

   c. Use a series of summary questions.

   d. Relate material to previously learned material.

   e. Have students demonstrate or apply the new material.

ACTIVITIES

1. *Television set induction techniques*   Watch the beginning of several television programs and observe how the concept of set induction is used to get viewers interested in the upcoming program. Can the same techniques be used by a teacher in a classroom environment?

2. *Listing of strategies*   Make a listing of the instructional strategies you feel are appropriate for the grade level you plan to teach. Give a valid rationale for your selection.

3. *Television closure techniques*   Watch the ending of several television programs and observe whether closure is achieved. If so, how?

4. *Planning a lesson*   Plan a lesson presentation for the topic of your choice from your area of specialization. Include in the plan the three key ingredients that make up a lesson presentation.

REFERENCES

Allen, D. W., et al. (1969). *Creating Student Involvement.* General Learning Corporation.

Ausubel, D. P. (1963). *The Psychology of Meaningful Verbal Learning: An Introduction to School Learning.* New York: Grune and Stratton.

Davis, O. L., Jr., et al. (1970). *Basic Teaching Tasks.* The University of Texas at Austin.

Hensen, K. T. (1981). *Secondary Teaching Methods.* Lexington, Mass.: D. C. Heath.

Kim, E. C., and Kellough, R. D. (1978). *A Resource Guide for Secondary School Teaching.* New York: Macmillan.

Orlich, D. C., et al. (1980). *Teaching Strategies.* Lexington, Mass.: D. C. Heath.

Peterson, P. L. (October 1979). Direct instruction: Effective for what and for whom? *Educational Leadership, 37,* 46–8.

Shostak, R. (1982). Lesson Presentation Skills. In *Classroom Teaching Skills: A Handbook,* 2d ed. Cooper, J. M., et al. Lexington, Mass.: D. C. Heath.

Planning the Evaluation

_____ OBJECTIVES

After completing your study of Chapter 5, you should be able to:

1. Explain the dual role served by the evaluation process
2. Explain the importance of evaluation in the learning process
3. Explain why evaluation should be a continual process
4. Explain the importance of evaluation in the affective domain
5. Compare and contrast formative and summative evaluation
6. Describe the four techniques that can be used to collect information for the evaluative process
7. Identify advantages and disadvantages of the different data collecting techniques
8. Identify and describe various evaluative instruments that can be used in the evaluative process
9. Identify advantages and disadvantages associated with the different evaluative instruments

All teachers must evaluate in order to determine where students are with respect to targeted learning objectives. If students have not mastered the intended material, reteaching must be planned. Viewed in this context, evaluation performs a dual role in the teaching-learning process. It gives the teacher information regarding the level of student learning, and it provides information that can be used in planning future lessons.

Being able to identify learner difficulties is a basic skill that successful teachers must possess. No matter how well you plan and implement your lessons, some students will probably experience difficulty in achieving the desired learning outcomes. Without proper identification and remediation, these difficulties may compound until the student becomes frustrated and turns off to learning altogether. Thus, evaluation and measurement are essential components in the teaching process.

Evaluation is the process of making a judgment regarding the student performance; **measurement** provides the data for making that judgment. Thus, evaluation is often more than simply measuring academic achievement. Sometimes you will be more interested in a student's performance than in the end product. This is particularly true when teaching psychomotor skills. For example you may want to evaluate how well your students participate in group work, how well they stay on an assigned task, or how they go about adjusting a microscope in an experiment. Also since attitudes and feelings often have a tremendous effect on learning, you should address such factors in your teaching and in your evaluation.

You teach to bring about learning. Consequently the ultimate question in the instructional process is whether or not your students have learned what they were supposed to learn. Can they display the outcomes specified in your original objectives? More specifically, do they meet the acceptable level of performance as specified in the criterion of your objectives? These objectives will call for the evaluation of cognitive skills, performance skills, and in some cases attitudes or feelings. Thus, evaluation can be required in the cognitive, psychomotor, and affective domains. These differences call for different evaluation techniques.

There are basically two types of evaluation: formative and summative (see Table 5.1). **Formative evaluation**, which is used to promote learning, takes place both before and during the learning process. It includes pretests, checkup tests that prompt students to study, observations of students' papers as they work, homework, and questioning during instruction. The results of formative evaluation should not be used to determine grades.

In contrast **summative evaluation** is an attempt to judge the extent of student learning and is often used to determine grades.

TABLE 5.1   Relationship between Formative and Summative Evaluation.

	FORMATIVE EVALUATION	SUMMATIVE EVALUATION
Purpose	To promote learning	To derive a grade
Nature	Few questions relative to specifics	Many questions relative to specific and general knowledge
Administered	Frequently—before or during instruction	Usually once at conclusion of instruction

Examples of summative evaluation are end-of-chapter tests, homework grades, completed project grades, and standardized achievement test scores.

Although such evaluative devices as homework and tests are most often used in summative evaluation, they can also be used to promote learning. Thus, some devices serve a dual function: to promote learning and to derive a grade.

Evaluation should be a continual process that includes both formative and summative goals. Many times you can gain valuable information regarding achievement, motor skills, or attitudes during the course of instruction. Difficulties may be noted, and if so, on-the-spot feedback provided to remedy the situation. For example lack of response to questioning can reveal that a concept is misunderstood. Trouble with a piece of lab equipment suggests that students need further instruction on its use. Or a spot check of childrens' papers during seatwork might reveal problem areas.

INFORMATION COLLECTING TECHNIQUES

Evaluation requires that a judgment be made, and this judgment requires information. TenBrink (1982) outlines four different techniques that can be used to gather information on student progress: observation, inquiry, analysis, and testing.

Observation

Observing your students not only tells you how well they are doing in specific areas, but it allows you to provide them with immediate feedback. Observational information is continuously available in the classroom as you watch and listen to students in numerous daily situations. A few such situations are:

1. *Oral reading.* Is the student having reading problems?

2. *Responding to questions.* Does the student understand the concepts?

3. *Following directions.* Does the student follow the given instructions?

4. *Group or seatwork.* Does the group stay on task?

5. *Interest in subject.* Does the student eagerly participate?

6. *Using resource materials.* Does the group correctly use materials in class?

Many educators criticize the use of observation in making evaluative judgments. They claim that it is too subjective and that the record keeping associated with observation is too time consuming. However, after teachers have refined their observational skills, these criticisms have little basis. First, concerns about subjectivity apply to all evaluation. Even pencil-and-paper tests involve subjectively choosing items for the test. The objectivity of observational information can also be greatly enhanced through the use of appropriate instrumentation. (We will address this issue later in the chapter.) Second, the time committed to observational record keeping can be kept under control if a file folder is kept for each student and a few descriptive phrases are added periodically. Examples might include such phrases as "Larry has difficulty remembering his multiplication facts," or "Alice must be continuously reinforced to stay on task," or "Ron has trouble with fine motor adjustments in physics lab."

Inquiry

Students themselves can often provide valuable evaluative information if you simply ask them how they feel, what they like or dislike, what they think, or how they did. Of course the reliability of the responses may be questionable since students, like most people, tend to tell you what they think you want to hear. Consequently inquiry should be used with care. A good way to improve reliability is to use observational skill in conjunction with inquiry.

Too many teachers think that only they can evaluate their students. However, if students are to learn to set their own goals, they can participate in the evaluative process in several ways. First, they can learn to check their own work as well as that of other students. You can assist in this self-evaluation process by providing a check list or the criteria against which the work is to be evaluated. Second, students can inspect their own work for strengths and weaknesses. For example, they could tape a speech, a class discussion, an oral report, or any practice materials and then critique the recorded material for strengths and weaknesses. Finally, they can often decide when they are ready to take a written exam or go on to something else. Whichever self-evaluative technique you decide to use, if any, it is usually unwise to include the evaluation in the student's final grade. Students will then be more realistic in their self-evaluations and will not be under pressure to distort their findings.

Analysis

Teachers grade or evaluate students' work on a regular basis, that is, they analyze it for possible errors. The analysis can take place either during or following instruction and, like the other techniques we have discussed, has the advantage of not being a formal test with its accompanying pressures. However, analysis is often more formal than observation and inquiry.

Analysis is important in that it provides early identification of learning difficulties. Immediate feedback can then be provided to remedy the difficulties. For example a science teacher might analyze and correct a student's lab techniques, an art teacher a student's painting technique, a second grade teacher a student's math seatwork, or a fifth grade teacher a student's written report. Whatever the nature of the work, you would be wise to file samples of the students' work for discussion at student and parent conferences.

Testing

Brown (1971, p. 8) defines a test as "a systematic procedure for measuring an individual's behavior." This definition implies that a test must be developed systematically (using specific guidelines) and must provide a procedure for responding, a criteria for scoring, and a description of student performance levels. Tests must be valid, reliable, and usable. **Validity** refers to the degree to which a test measures what it is meant to measure. It tells you the degree to which the test is fulfilling its function. For example a measurement of height would not give a valid measure of weight. Test **reliability** is the consistency with which the test measures whatever it measures, that is, the consistency of scores obtained by the same person when retested with the identical or an equivalent form of the test. A bathroom scale that does not give a consistent weight measure is not reliable. Finally, **usability** refers to practical considerations such as cost, time to administer, difficulty, and scoring procedure. For example a two-hour exam would not be very usable for a one-hour exam period.

Although most tests are developed to measure cognitive achievement, some are used to measure attitudes, feelings, and motor skills. However, due to problems associated with validity, reliability, and usability, one must use extra care in selecting tests that measure attitudes and motor skills.

Testing, like other evaluative techniques, has certain limitations. Too often tests fail to provide the information that is most important in the evaluation of the students. For example most tests do not measure student motivation, physical limitations, or environmental factors. In addition teachers must guard against tests that are improperly constructed, poorly administered, and vulnerable to student guessing. Also by their very nature, pencil-and-paper tests are more likely to test knowing rather than thinking abilities, verbalizations rather than doing, and teacher wants rather than true attitudes or feelings. However, with care tests can be developed to assess thinking ability. The problem is that most teachers lack either the time or the expertise to construct proper tests. Consequently, you must often use other devices, which will be discussed later in this chapter, to supplement formal pencil-and-paper tests.

Testing is probably the most common measurement technique used by teachers, but it may not be the most important. Testing should be thought of as only one of several techniques that you can use to obtain information about student progress.

Table 5.2 gives a comparison of the four evaluative techniques we have discussed. Study the table and then complete Tasks 5.1 and 5.2.

TABLE 5.2 Comparison of Information Collecting Techniques.

	INQUIRY	OBSERVATION	ANALYSIS	TESTING
Kind of information obtainable	Opinions Affective attributes Attitudes Feelings	Performance Products Affective attributes (especially emotional reactions) Social skills Behavior	Learning outcomes Cognitive and psycho-motor skills Affective outcomes	Attitude and achievement Cognitive outcomes
Objectivity	Least objective Highly subject to error	Subjective but can be objective if instruments are used	Objective but not stable over time	Most objective and reliable

SOURCE: Adapted from Terry D. TenBrink (1974), *Evaluation: A Practical Guide for Teachers.* New York: McGraw-Hill, p. 140.

TASK 5.1   Collecting Information

Answer the following questions. Check your responses with those given at the end of the chapter.

1. Give the two uses of teacher collected information.

   a. _____

   _____

   b. _____

   _____

2. Summative evaluation is most often used to promote learning. (True/False)

3. Describe the four techniques that can be used to obtain evaluative information.

   a. _____

   _____

   b. _____

   _____

   c. _____

   _____

   d. _____

   _____

4. The use of observation is too often a poor evaluative technique. (True/False)

5. Only teachers should make judgments regarding student progress. (True/False)

6. The most objective and reliable information is provided through testing.   (True/False)

TASK 5.2   Identifying Information Collecting Techniques

Following is a series of questions that requires you to collect information. Indicate whether observation (0), inquiry (I), analysis (A), or testing (T) is the best technique for collecting the information. Check your responses with those given at the end of the chapter.

_____	1.	Why is Mark's group always last in finishing assigned tasks?
_____	2.	What are the common errors on the algebra assignment?
_____	3.	Does the class like the poetry we have been studying?
_____	4.	Has the class learned what was taught about foreign lands?
_____	5.	Has the class learned to appreciate the place of science in our society?
_____	6.	Can the students correctly write a research paper?
_____	7.	Which students are having trouble with social skills?
_____	8.	Which students know all their spelling words?
_____	9.	What are the class problem areas on pronouncing the new vocabulary words?
_____	10.	What would the students like to study next semester?

EVALUATIVE INSTRUMENTS

Some form of data recording instrument must be available if teachers are to systematically use the data gathering techniques just described. And since evaluation is a continual process, you should not rely on just one device to gain information regarding students' progress. Consequently we will discuss in this section the general characteristics of five evaluation devices. Whereas guidelines for constructing the devices are beyond the scope of this book, we recommend that you take coursework or read a basic textbook that deals with the construction of evaluation instruments. Let us now examine some of the evaluative options.

Standardized Tests

Mehens and Lehmann (1975) define **standardized test** as one that is commercially developed and samples behavior under uniform procedures. Uniform procedures mean that the same questions are administered to students with the same directions, the time limit for taking the test is the same for everyone, and the results are scored using a carefully detailed procedure.

The procedure for the development of a standardized test is quite complex. First, specialists write a series of questions about a particular subject or battery of subjects; the questions should be answerable by the well-informed student at a particular grade level. Next, the questions are tried out on a representative sample of students at that grade level from all kinds of schools in all parts of the country. Based on feedback from the representative sample, the test is revised and arranged in the final version of the exam. The exam is then administered to a sample of students that is larger and more carefully selected to represent the target grade level. These students form the norming group against which all subsequent scores are compared. This procedure makes it possible to compare the performance of a particular student against a larger group of students or to compare the performance of one group of students against another group. Thus, you could compare school districts, compare a single school district's students with all students in a state, or compare students in a state with all students in the nation.

Standardized tests come in several forms. Some are used to measure knowledge in specific areas, such as arithmetic, reading, English, social studies, or chemistry. These tests are usually referred to as **achievement tests**, since they measure how much a student has learned in a particular area or battery of areas. Other standardized tests are designed to measure students' aptitudes or abilities for performing certain activities. These tests are designed to measure a person's potential in a given field, such as science, mathematics, drafting, auto mechanics, or law, and are given a variety of labels including *scholastic aptitude tests, general ability tests,* and *intelligence tests.*

The major reason for using standardized achievement tests in the classroom is to supplement teacher evaluation. The tests can give valuable information regarding how well your students are doing in comparison with other local or national student groups.

There are also certain limitations associated with the use of standardized tests. First, they are expensive to administer. Second, their validity is questionable in situations where they do not measure what was taught, that is, they may not be consistent with the teacher's goals and objectives. Finally, a standardized test is likely to have some cultural bias, which means the test may discriminate against certain cultural groups that lack prerequisite language, background experience, or testing experience.

Teacher-Made Tests

Teacher-made tests are the most popular of all evaluative instruments. They differ from standardized tests in that they are constructed by the classroom teacher to meet particular needs and, if properly constructed, are usually consistent with classroom goals and objectives. In addition they are much less expensive to administer.

Offsetting these advantages, however, is the fact that many classroom teachers lack the skill to design valid tests or write appropriate test items. Although the validity of many teacher-made tests is questionable, they are an important part of the instructional process. Consequently you should develop and refine your skill in test construction.

Teachers also develop and use classroom quizzes to evaluate student progress. Teacher quizzes differ from regular teacher-made tests in that they are usually short, three to five questions, and they are usually limited to the material taught in the immediate or preceding lesson. The main purpose of teacher quizzes is to see what concepts from the preceding lesson the students have not grasped or perhaps have misunderstood.

Rating Scales

As noted earlier, observations can be an effective evaluative technique. However, they often lack reliability and validity. For example, teachers can view students differently, let the time of day effect their observation, or allow their perceptions to change with time. These defects can be overcome to some extent through the use of rating scales, checklists, or some other written guide to help objectify one's observations. Let us look first at the design and use of rating scales.

Rating scales can be extremely helpful in judging skills, products, procedures, social behaviors, and attitudes. A rating scale is nothing more than a series of categories that is arranged in order of quality. For example a scale for using the backhand in tennis might have five steps, with the lowest category labeled inadequate and the top labeled proficient. It might look like this:

| 0 | 1 | 2 | 3 | 4 | 5 |
| inadequate | | | | | proficient |

The rater would develop the criteria for what to look for in the proper use of the backhand and mark students on their use of it. Other scales might be prepared for effective use of the forehand, the serve, the lob, and the ability to volley. The total instrument might be similar to the one shown in Figure 5.1.

Scales similar to those presented in Figure 5.1 can be developed for observations of a student product, of social behaviors, or of attitudes. One need only change the attributes being judged and perhaps change the low and high scale classification. If applicable,

FIGURE 5.1 Rating Scale for Tennis. An X is placed on each scale to represent the student's skill on the attribute.

Rating Scale: Tennis

Name _____ Date _____

Directions: Rate the student's performance on each tennis skill by placing an X on the appropriate position on the scale.

1. Serve

| • — • — • — • — • — • |
| 0   1   2   3   4   5 |
| inadequate   adequate |

2. Forehand

| • — • — • — • — • — • |
| 0   1   2   3   4   5 |
| inadequate   adequate |

3. Backhand

| • — • — • — • — • — • |
| 0   1   2   3   4   5 |
| inadequate   adequate |

4. Lob

| • — • — • — • — • — • |
| 0   1   2   3   4   5 |
| inadequate   adequate |

5. Volley

| • — • — • — • — • — • |
| 0   1   2   3   4   5 |
| inadequate   adequate |

---

you might want to change the zero-to-five scale values shown in Figure 5.1 to a more appropriate scale value, such as this:

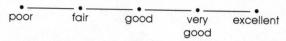

poor   fair   good   very   excellent
                        good

Rating scales allow observers to separate a total performance into various subskills and, with appropriate scale judgments, the quality of a student's performance can be better determined. The results are more valid and reliable observations. However, some uncertainty will still exist.

Check Lists

A check list differs from a rating scale in that it indicates the presence or absence of specified characteristics. A **check list** is basically a list of the criteria upon which a student's performance or end product is to be judged. You use the check list by simply checking off those criteria items that have been met.

The type of response for each entry on a check list can vary. It can be as simple as a check mark indicating that a listed action has occurred. For example a check list for observing student participation in group work might look like this:

_____ 1. Starts work promptly

_____ 2. Displays interest in work

_____ 3. Cooperates with others

_____ 4. Makes worthwhile suggestions

The rater would simply check those items that occurred during group work.

Another type of check list that is sometimes used requires a yes or no response. The yes is checked when the action has been performed in a satisfactory manner; the no is checked when the action has been unsatisfactory. An example of this type of check list used in a speech class is shown in Figure 5.2. The rater would check the appropriate column on each item as to whether the performance level has been met.

The development and use of check lists sensitizes the observer to the various parts of desired actions. By getting more reliable data on the component parts, the observer is better able to evaluate the overall performance.

FIGURE 5.2 Performance Check List for a Speech Class.

Performance Check List: Speech

Name _____Date _____

Directions: Check **Yes** or **No** as to whether criterion level is met.

Did the student:	Yes	No
1. Use correct grammar	_____	_____
2. Make clear presentation	_____	_____
3. Stimulate interest	_____	_____
4. Use clear diction	_____	_____
5. Show poise	_____	_____
6. Reveal enthusiasm	_____	_____
7. Use appropriate voice projection	_____	_____

Questionnaires

Attitudes, feelings, and opinions are admittedly difficult to evaluate. For some attitudinal goals, long-time observation may be needed since representative behaviors may not occur on a daily basis. A common technique for overcoming this difficulty is the use of a pupil **questionnaire**, which requires students to examine themselves and react to a series of statements regarding their attitudes, feelings, and opinions. The author of the questionnaire decides what information is wanted and then designs statements or questions that will elicit this information.

The response style on questionnaires can vary from a simple check list-type response to open-ended statements. Whenever possible you should design questionnaires so that they call for short answers only.

The check list-type response usually provides students with a list of adjectives for describing or evaluating something and instructs them to check those that apply. For example a checklist questionnaire on the attitude of students in a mathematics class might include such statements as:

1. This class is

   _____ exciting.

   _____ boring.

   _____ interesting.

   _____ unpleasant.

   _____ informative.

2. I find mathematics

   _____ fun.

   _____ interesting.

   _____ a drudgery.

   _____ difficult.

   _____ easy.

The scoring of this type of test is simple. You subtract the number of negative statements checked from the number of positive statements checked. The result is the positiveness of the attitude.

A second type of response cycle that can be used on questionnaires is often referred to as the semantic differential. A **semantic differential** is usually a seven-point scale that links an adjective to its opposite. The semantic differential response is designed so that attitudes, feelings, and opinions can be measured by degrees, from

very favorable to highly unfavorable. Examples from a questionnaire that could be used to check students' attitudes toward
science might look like this:

Science Is

interesting _____ : _____ : _____ : _____ : _____ : _____ : _____ boring

  pleasant _____ : _____ : _____ : _____ : _____ : _____ : _____ unpleasant

    good _____ : _____ : _____ : _____ : _____ : _____ : _____ bad

The composite score on the total questionnaire is determined by
averaging the scale values given to all items included on the instrument.

One of the most frequently used response styles in attitude
measurement is the **Likert Scale**, which is usually a five-point
scale that links the options "strongly agree" and "strongly
disagree" as follows:

```
•_____•_____•_____•_____•
strongly        agree      undecided    disagree    strongly
agree                                                disagree
```

The students respond to statements by checking the options that
most closely represent their feelings about the statements. An example of this type of instrument is shown in Figure 5.3. The Link-
ert Scale is usually scored by assigning a value of one to five to the
available options. Five is usually assigned to the option "strongly
agree" and one to the option "strongly disagree." These assigned
values are usually reversed when the statement is negative. The
composite score is then determined by adding all the scale values.

Another type of response style that can be used on questionnaires is sentence completion. Partial sentences are presented,
and students are asked to complete them with words that best express their feelings, for example:

I find biology to be_____.

This class is _____.

The responses are then scored as to content for each respondent.

The advantages in using questionnaires are that they can be administered in a relatively short period, they can often be used to
help students improve their vocabulary, they can help students
clarify their feelings, and they are generally easy to score. However, there are also disadvantages. One cannot be absolutely sure
true feelings are being expressed, and they are often too complex
for young children.

This concludes our formal discussion of evaluative instruments. Complete Tasks 5.3 and 5.4, which were designed to test
your understanding of the material.

FIGURE 5.3 Attitude Scale for Determining Students' Attitude toward the Metric System.

Attitude Scale: The Metric System

Name _____Date _____

Each of the statements below expresses a feeling toward the metric system. Rate each statement on the extent to which you agree. For each you may strongly agree (A), agree (B), be undecided (C), disagree (D), or strongly disagree (E).

•—————•—————•—————•—————•
strongly   agree   undecided   disagree   strongly
agree   disagree

_____ 1. The metric system is fun to use.

_____ 2. I don't like the metric system. It scares me to use it.

_____ 3. The metric system is easy to understand.

_____ 4. In general I have good feelings toward the metric system.

_____ 5. I approach the metric system with hesitation.

_____ 6. I feel at ease in using the metric system.

_____ 7. The metric system makes me feel uncomfortable, irritable, and impatient.

_____ 8. I feel a definite positive reaction to the metric system.

TASK 5.3 Evaluation Instruments

Answer the following questions. Check your responses with those given at the end of the chapter.

1. List five evaluative devices that can be used in the classroom.

    a. _____

    b. _____

    c. _____

    d. _____

    e. _____

2. All standardized tests are achievement tests.　(True/False)

3. The best evaluative device to use when comparing groups is a standardized test.　(True/False)

4. The best evaluative device to use for the measurement of classroom goals and objectives is the teacher-made test.　(True/False)

5. A rating scale is used to indicate the presence or absence of a specified attribute.   (True/False)

6. A commonly used device for determining attitudes, feelings, and opinions is the questionnaire.   (True/False)

TASK 5.4 Identifying Evaluation Instruments

A series of situations that require evaluation follows. Please indicate the best evaluation instrument to use in each situation: achievement test (A), teacher-made test (T), rating scale (R), check list (C), or questionnaire (Q). Check your responses with those given at the end of the chapter.

_____ 1. A third grade teacher wants to know whether students' cursive writing has improved.

_____ 2. An eighth grade teacher wants to know how students feel about the poetry unit.

_____ 3. A school district superintendent wants to know how students in the district are doing compared to students in the state.

_____ 4. A drivers education teacher wants to know whether students are following the correct procedure for starting a car.

_____ 5. A mathematics teacher just finished teaching a unit on polygons and wants to know if the material was mastered.

_____ 6. An art teacher wants to determine how well students can draw a series of figures.

_____ 7. A fifth grade teacher wants to know how her students compare with other students in reading.

_____ 8. A shop teacher wants to know the woodworking tools preferred by students.

SUMMARY

Evaluation is an essential tool for teachers because it gives them feedback concerning what their students have learned and indicates what should be done next in the learning process. Evaluation helps you to better understand students, their abilities, interests, attitudes, and needs in order to better teach and motivate them.

There are two types of evaluation: formative and summative. Formative evaluation is most often used prior to and during instruction to promote learning, while summative evaluation follows instruction and is most often used to judge the end product of learning.

To carry out the various functions served by evaluation you must develop skill in selecting the best data gathering technique and the best data recording instrument. You must develop an understanding of the advantages and disadvantages of such evaluative techniques as observation, analysis, inquiry, and testing.

Once you have chosen a data gathering technique, you must be able to select an appropriate instrument for recording valid and reliable data. This selection will usually be related to the specific domain under study. The desired data may require measurement in the cognitive domain (achievement), the psychomotor domain (process or performance), or the affective domain (attitudes, feelings, or opinions). Measurement in the cognitive domain usually requires a test (achievement or teacher made) or some type of written work, whereas measurement of processes and performances are usually best carried out through the use of rating scales and check lists. Measurement of attitudes, feelings, and options are the most difficult to obtain and are usually best measured through observations or through the use of questionnaires.

Answer Keys

TASK 5.1 Collecting Information

1. a. Gives the level of student achievement.
   b. Helps determine content of future lessons.

2. *False* Summative evaluation is most often used to judge the final product of learning.

3. a. Observation of students in the learning environment.
   b. The use of inquiry. This consists of simply asking students for the desired information.
   c. Analyze student work for errors.
   d. Test students over information taught.

4. *False* Some educators criticize the use of observation due to its subjective nature. But if used correctly, observation can provide useful information.

5. *False* It is often desirable and effective to have students judge their own work.

6. *True* Tests provide the most objective and reliable information, whereas inquiry provides the least objective information.

TASK 5.2   Identifying Information Collecting Techniques

1. *O*   Observe the group to see what is delaying them.
2. *A*   Analyze the students' work.
3. *A or I*   Observe student reaction to the poetry or simply ask them.
4. *T*   A test will tell you what they know.
5. *I*   Ask them.
6. *A*   Give them an assignment and analyze the results.
7. *O*   Observe students in social situations.
8. *T*   Give the students a spelling test.
9. *O*   Listen to students.
10. *I*   Ask them.

TASK 5.3   Evaluation Instruments

1. a. Standardized tests
   b. Teacher-made tests
   c. Rating scales
   d. Check lists
   e. Questionnaires
2. *False*   Standardized tests can be aptitude tests, general ability tests, or intelligence tests.
3. *True*   Standardized tests are normed and, therefore, can be used to compare groups.
4. *True*   Teacher-made tests should be written to measure the classroom goals and objectives.
5. *False*   A check list is used to indicate the presence or absence of a specified attribute.
6. *True*   Questionnaires overcome many of the difficulties associated with the measurement of attitudes, feelings, and opinions.

TASK 5.4   Identifying Evaluation Instruments

1. *R*   Rate students on their cursive writing skill.
2. *Q*   Design a questionnaire on poetry and have students respond.
3. *A*   Compare achievement test scores.
4. *C*   List the procedure to be followed and check for each student.
5. *T*   Design a test on the material covered.
6. *R*   Design a scale for each figure and rate students on each.
7. *A*   Compare reading achievement test scores.
8. *C*   List tools and check those used by students.

ACTIVITIES

1. *Evaluation information*   Information to be utilized in evaluation can be collected through observation, inquiry, analysis, and testing. Make a listing of at least five kinds of information that can be collected through the use of each of the four data collecting techniques. Submit the listing to your instructor.

2. *Class evaluation*   For a hypothetical class, list data collection techniques and evaluative devices that you could use to evaluate cognitive growth, attitudes, and psychomotor skills.

3. *Rating scale development*   Develop a rating scale that could be used to assist you in judging the social behaviors you desire in a classroom. If possible, use the scale in an actual classroom setting.

4. *Check list development*   Develop a check list that could be used to evaluate a student's performance in carrying out a task of your choice. If possible, use the check list in a classroom setting.

5. *Self-assessment*   Discuss the importance of student self-assessment. Outline three procedures or techniques that could be used for self-assessment by students.

REFERENCES

Ahmann, J. S., and Glock, M. D. (1981). *Evaluating Student Progress.* Boston: Allyn and Bacon.

Brown, F. G. (1971). *Measurement and Evaluation.* Itasca, Ill.: F. E. Peacock.

Hills, J. R. (1981). *Measurement and Evaluation in the Classroom,* 2d ed. Columbus, Ohio: Charles E. Merrill.

Mehrens, W., and Lehmann, I. (1975). *Standardized Tests in Evaluation.* New York: Holt, Rinehart, and Winston.

TenBrink, T. D. (1974). *Evaluation: A Practical Guide for Teachers.* New York: McGraw Hill.

TenBrink, T. D. (1982). Evaluation. In *Classroom Teaching Skills,* 2d ed. Cooper, J. M., et al. Lexington, Mass.: D. C. Heath.

_____ part 3

INSTRUCTIONAL SKILLS

Once planned, your lessons must be implemented, and this requires that you master a variety of teaching skills. First, you must be able to communicate effectively. Second, you must be able to establish and maintain student attention. Third, you must be able to elicit responses from your students to keep them involved and to examine the results of your teaching. Finally, you must be an effective classroom manager.

Part 3 will assist you in the development and refinement of these skills. Chapter 6 addresses the most important skill, communications. It looks at techniques associated with both verbal and nonverbal communications and takes a close look at the often overlooked but important skill of listening. Chapters 7, 8, and 9 address those skills that will assist you in keeping students involved in their lessons. The topics covered include stimulus variation, reinforcement, and questioning. Chapter 10 discusses classroom management. We will look at leadership and classroom atmosphere and their effect on behavior as well as several commonly used models of discipline.

Communication

After completing your study of Chapter 6, you should be able to:

1. Explain the importance of the communication process
2. Differentiate between the verbal and vocal components of a message
3. Identify variables associated with the verbal and vocal components of a message
4. Explain the role nonverbal communication holds in the communication process
5. List and describe various nonverbal behaviors that are commonly used in teaching-learning situations
6. Explain the importance of listening to the communication process
7. Identify and describe variables that interfere with the listening process
8. Define and explain the reflective listening process
9. Explain the importance of feedback in the communication process

Without communication teaching and learning could not occur. Teachers therefore are intimately involved in the communication process as they interact with students on a daily basis. Teachers continually send messages to students and receive messages from them (see Figure 6.1).

As shown in Figure 6.1, communication can be viewed as a four-phase process. First, the sender encodes (composes) a message into a form which will hopefully be understood by the receiver and then transmits this message. The transmitted message is received and decoded by a receiver who then encodes some form of reaction to the message. The reaction is often nonverbal and is used to communicate whether the message was understood or not. The receiver sends the encoded reaction back to the sender who then decodes and reacts to the feedback. The sender's reaction to the feedback may be to continue with new information, to clarify the original message, or to repeat the message.

A typical classroom situation serves to illustrate the communication process. Suppose you want to communicate the importance of a specific point to your students and encode and send a message such as "This is a point worth remembering." The transmitted message is received and decoded by students as meaning the information will probably be on the next exam. They add it to their notes. Since you see (feedback) the information included in the students' notes, you feel you have communicated the importance of the information and continue with new information. However, if you see that the students do not add the information, you might want to encode and send another message such as "This point is so important that I think I will repeat it!" This example shows the

FIGURE 6.1 The Communication Process.   A four-phase process.

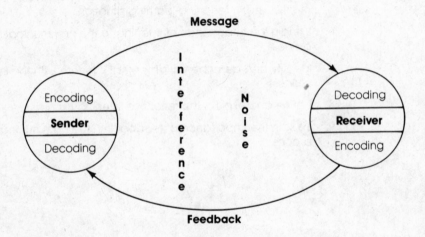

importance of encoding your messages so that they are decoded accurately by students, and it shows the importance of feedback in the communication process. Noise and interference are usually present during the communication process; they must be overcome if messages are to be received and decoded accurately.

Messages may be sent or received through verbal, vocal, physical, or situational stimuli. As a teacher you must be skilled at sending and receiving messages through all these modes. Your ability to decode messages (feedback) transmitted by students depends directly on your skill at observing and listening. We discussed making accurate observations in Chapter 2. The three skills that we will examine here are verbal communication, nonverbal communication, and skill at listening.

Most teacher preparatory programs stress reading and writing in their communication curriculum. Little emphasis is put on speaking, and almost no attention is given to nonverbal communication and the skill of listening. However, the most persuasive and effective teachers do not rely exclusively on reading and writing; they talk, they observe, and they listen with equal skill.

VERBAL COMMUNICATION

Teachers talk in order to convey information. Unfortunately learning does not always result from teacher talk. Nonverbal variables often determine whether or not something is learned.

Hennings (1975, p. 3) breaks spoken messages into verbal and vocal components. The **verbal component** includes the actual words spoken and their meanings, while the **vocal component** includes such variables as voice firmness, modulation, tone, tempo, pitch, and loudness. We shall now take a closer look at each of these two components.

Verbal Learning

What is learned in a verbal interaction depends on the meanings attached to the spoken words by the learner. The meanings vary according to the unique experiences through which each learner filters the words. For example a discussion of the importance of school or a discussion of dentists will have varying meanings for students depending on their past experiences. Despite language conventions and formal definitions, you must make sure that your verbal instruction is related as much as possible to the unique experiences of your students. This calls for an assessment of what your students bring to the learning situation, for example, intelligence, prior experiences, and learning ability. This assessment may show that the verbal aspects of your messages are outside the experience base of your students. (A word of caution: Do not let your assessment of students color your expectation of their ability. Students tend to perform up or down to their teacher's expectations.)

Hurt, Scott, and McCrosky (1978, p. 76) suggest several other variables which are related to the verbal component of a message and may have some effect on whether the message is learned. These variables include:

1. *Organization.*   Good or well-organized verbal information tends to be learned better. Also information presented at the beginning or end of a message tends to be retained better.

2. *Message sidedness.*   Two-sided messages, that is, messages that present opposing views, tend to be learned best.

3. *Language intensity.*   Verbal information that deviates from a neutral position appears to be learned better.

4. *Concreteness and ambiguity.*   The more concrete a message, the better it is learned. However, the message must not be made so concrete that the basic concept is lost.

Generally such variables as those discussed earlier and those suggested by Hurt, Scott, and McCraskey tend to increase the attention of the learner and thereby increase learning.

Vocal Learning

The human voice can bring words to life. Changes in voice loudness, pitch, inflection, tone, and rate not only affect the emphasis within messages but can actually change the meaning of words. For example, "Come here!" or "Sit down!" can convey different meanings depending on voice loudness, pitch, and tone.

Although everyone is not endowed with a strong voice that projects well, teachers must learn to interact with groups and to emphasize points with their voice. It is essential that you learn to vary the strength of your voice and to project it so that it can be heard by all members of the class. This takes practice, but is well worth the effort. Simple exercises that involve talking over a little distance or consciously inhaling and exhaling air will improve both the strength and projection of your voice.

The rate at which you speak is important as well. When someone speaks rapidly, it often conveys the unintended message that the subject is not really important and should be completed as soon as possible. In contrast words spoken at a slower rate often communicate their importance and invite careful attention. This is important to remember since you might be required to teach subjects in which you have little personal interest or preparation. With these subjects you must take care to watch your rate of presentation.

The tone, inflection, and pitch of the voice often affects a message. Tone or inflection can communicate word seriousness or validity. For example your tone and inflection will communicate your seriousness when you make such statements as, "I mean it! Sit down!" or "I am losing my patience with this class!" Moreover, as Hennings (1975, p. 17) points out, "The high-pitched voice can grate on a decoder's nerves so that the listener turns off to words spoken; the very deep voice can distract from the message." You must, therefore, guard against using a tone, inflection, or pitch that detracts from your message.

Voice loudness, rate, tone, inflection, and pitch can also send emotional messages. Loudness, fast rate, and uneven pitch communicate excitement or enthusiasm, whereas a slow rate and even pitch sometimes communicate disinterest. Joy, eagerness, anger, wonder, awe, displeasure, determination, and indecisiveness are communicated through variations in the voice. Skill at using your voice can greatly assist you in keeping students on task, in maintaining a positive classroom environment, and in preventing a loss of student attention. Practice the effective use of your voice and, above all, watch your students for feedback. It will pay dividends.

To reinforce your understanding of how the voice can affect communication, complete Task 6.1.

TASK 6.1   Verbal Communication

Observe a conversation between several people around you or on a television talk show. Listen to both the verbal component (the words) and the vocal component (the manner in which they are spoken) of participants in the conversation and note below any discrepancy between the two. Record below any vocal messages (excitement, interest, fear, etc.) you observe being sent and the voice qualities (tone, pitch, rate, etc.) used to send these messages.

The recorded observations for this task will vary considerably. However, some possible observations are listed at the end of the chapter.

Differences between Verbal and Vocal Communication

1. Difference_____

2. Difference_____

3. Difference_____

4. Difference_____

5. Difference_____

Vocal Messages Communicated

Vocal Messages	Voice Qualities Used

NONVERBAL COMMUNICATION

Not all communication is audible. Of special importance to teachers is nonverbal communication, which according to the estimates
of some researchers, accounts for over 80 percent of our total communication.

We constantly send messages through our postures, the way we
look, stand, move, use our voice, dress, and use space, as well as
the way we use words. These nonverbal messages can reinforce,
modify, or even contradict our verbal messages as, for example,
when a vacant, half-hearted smile accompanies a rote welcome
such as, ''Hello. It's so nice to see you.'' In fact sometimes the
nonverbal part of communication is more important than the verbal part. We often use the nonverbal information we receive in
deciding what our reaction or role will be in a certain situation.
For example your host may ask you to stay longer, but his posture, look, and voice suggest that he would much rather you
leave. Actions do often speak louder than words.

Nonverbal communication can be accidental, or it can be planned and managed. Either way, nonverbal cues influence perceptions and attitudes. Rather than taking them at face value, we
often use them as the basis of inferences we make about each
other or situations. Teachers and students often unwittingly reveal

attitudes and feelings toward each other and school in general through nonverbal cues. You must be aware of your nonverbal expressions and the effect they can have on students. Awareness is the first step toward controlling nonverbal expressions, a difficult but manageable task. We will now look at some nonverbal languages.

Facial Language

According to Miller (1981), the face is second only to words in communicating internal feelings. Miller further suggests that facial expressions can be readily visible or fleeting, involuntary or voluntary. Whatever the type, it should be remembered that facial expressions can reinforce, modify, or even contradict the spoken word.

Readily visible facial expressions are usually intentional. They are used to send a message (e.g., a smile indicating pleasure) or to mask our true feelings (e.g., a poker face hiding displeasure). These expressions are formed by movement of the facial muscles as, for example, wrinkling the forehead to communicate deep thought, lifting the eyebrows to reveal wonder or surprise, sneering to show anger, and jutting the chin to show firmness. Fleeting facial expressions on the other hand are often unintentional and are quickly covered up with other expressions. For example we may feel sudden disgust, anger, or dislike for someone which we do not want to communicate to the individual. We quickly mask our true feelings with other expressions.

Involuntary facial expressions usually take place under highly emotional circumstances in which we are fearful, angry, happy, or surprised. In learning environments these expressions are often fleeting and are quickly covered up with other expressions. However, under certain circumstances you may want to retain these expressions to convey a message to students. For example teachers often use expressions of anger to control misbehaving students and use expressions of humor to relieve tension or to improve student attention.

Teacher have learned to use certain expressions to convey specific messages. Familiar examples include the smile of approval and the frown of disapproval.

The use of the eyes is probably the most meaningful channel of nonverbal communication available to us. As Miller (1981, p. 14) points out, our eyes "can be shifty and evasive, conveying hate, fear, and guilt, or they can express confidence, love, and support." Also with eye contact we can open communication, prolong communication, or cut off communication.

Teachers often use eye contact to control interaction in the classroom. When they want a student to speak they make direct eye contact with him or her. Conversely, when they want to continue talking they avoid direct eye contact with anyone who may want to speak. In addition teachers sometimes use eye contact to determine which students may not answer a question, which students have not completed their homework, or which students may be lying. The stereotype has it that when we have not done as we should or when we are lying, we avoid direct eye contact. However, this stereotype has not been proven by research.

Direct eye contact—a stare—can also be used to change behavior. A stare used in conjunction with silence can be quite useful in gaining the attention of misbehaving or inattentive students. The stare alone often results in appropriate student behavior.

Body Language

Gestures with the head, arms, hands, and other body parts are pervasive nonverbal communicators. Gestures may describe, as when we form a model in the air with our hands; they may reinforce, as when we nod our head when someone is speaking; they may emphasize a point, as when we tap something we have written on the chalkboard; they may gain attention, as when we rap the desk or stomp our foot. Each of these actions physically communicates some type of information. However, you should take care not to overuse gestures. When a speaker uses too many gestures, the listener cannot really tell what is important in the message. Overuse can also result in a listener's attending to the gestures rather than the message. In short watch your students and ask questions. If students appear to be attending more to your gestures than to your messages, curtail the use of some gestures.

Your stance and general posture can also communicate information. A tense body tends to communicate closedness and insecurity. A relaxed torso or relaxed limbs tend to denote strength, openness, and friendliness. The orientation of a speaker's body, that is, the degree to which the speaker's body faces the listener, can also communicate information. A more direct orientation suggests a liking for the audience and a feeling of security in the communication process.

The use of touch is a very powerful nonverbal communicator. However, for teachers communication through touch is directly related to the age of the student. It is usually a necessary communicator with primary age children but inappropriate with upper elementary and secondary age students.

Younger children in the primary grades have a strong need for touch and physical contact with the teacher. The physical contact is needed to form a sense of belonging, security, and a caring relationship. Withholding contact can communicate rejection or dislike for a child. Remember that a hug or a pat on the back is a good reinforcer for the young child.

With secondary students touching should usually be avoided. However, a pat on the back for a job well done can sometimes be appropriate even with students at this age. Although it is usually unwise for a teacher to touch a student of the opposite sex, it can sometimes be used effectively. You should use your best judgment whether to communicate by touch with older students or with students of the opposite sex.

The Language of Space and Motion

How you use space and arrange your learning environment can also communicate a message. Where and how you choose to move within the confines of the learning environment, as well as how you arrange objects within that environment, are significant.

Learning environments are often territorial. The teacher's desk forms the teacher's territory, and each student's seat or desk forms the individual student's territory. In such an arrangement, it is often understood that neither is to invade the other's territory. This arrangement too often restricts classroom interaction and feelings of openness and may lead to a feeling of separation between teacher and students.

Teacher movement during interaction can aid or hinder the communication process. Teacher movement toward a speaker conveys a message of interest, whereas teacher movement away from a speaker communicates lack of interest. This movement, then, can result in termination of the communication process or it can prolong the process.

The physical makeup of the learning environment creates moods and affects the interaction within the environment. These findings are pointed out by Miller (1981, p. 24) in his summary of research related to student reactions in ugly and beautiful classrooms. He reports that "subjects in the ugly room had reactions of monotony, fatigue, headaches, irritability, and hostility, while subjects in the beautiful room responded favorably with feelings of comfort, pleasure, importance, and enjoyment for completing the assigned tasks." These findings tend to suggest that a well-decorated, pleasing environment is more conducive to open communication and learning.

The Language of Time

How a teacher decides to use class time communicates important information. Spending little time on a topic or passing it by often communicates that the topic is unimportant or that the teacher has little interest in it. Unless care is taken, this same attitude can unintentionally be instilled in students.

Pauses represent another way time can be used to enhance communication. Pausing just before or just after a specific point is presented signifies the importance of the topic. Teacher pauses can cue students that an important point is going to be made or that the last point was important and the students should think about it. Longer pauses can reflect anxiety, intimacy, or an attempt to mask uncertainty or fear.

Teachers ask students many questions in the course of a day's instruction. However, teachers often find it difficult to wait a sufficient time for student responses. Too often teachers expect instant answers to their questions and when not forthcoming, tend to answer the questions themselves. If these teachers were to increase the time they wait for a response (wait time), they would find improved communication in the classroom. The subject of wait time is further developed in Chapter 9.

The Language of the Voice

As noted earlier, we often send messages vocally, that is, through voice intonations. Intonations subtly reveal many things about a speaker, such as hidden prejudices, strong emotions and beliefs and, often, information about the speaker, such as socioeconomic background, level of education, and place of birth.

The adage, "It's not what we say, but how we say it that counts," is true. If a teacher responds to a student statement with "Very good!" (with rising intonation), it conveys a different message from a simple, monotone "Very good." The latter response conveys the message that it really was not that good. As pointed out earlier, when such contradictions occur between a verbal and vocal message, the latter is usually believed.

Clearly, different vocal intonations communicate different meanings. A message can be changed by varying loudness and softness, using high pitch or low pitch, or by varying the tone or quality of speech. You must understand and pay attention to the effect these voice intonations have on the meaning of your messages. You must learn to speak so there is congruence between your verbal and vocal messages.

Task 6.2 gives you more experience at identifying the various methods and messages that can be communicated through nonverbal communications. Complete the task and discuss your observations with fellow observers.

This concludes our discussion of verbal and nonverbal communications. In the next section, we consider another very important topic related to the communication process, the art of listening. However, before going on, check your understanding of the material just presented by completing Task 6.3.

TASK 6.2   Nonverbal Communication

Watch and listen to an interaction episode between several people around you or on a television talk show. Note examples of nonverbal communication that fall into each of the categories listed and briefly describe the meaning of each. Although the responses will vary considerably, possible examples are given at the end of the chapter.

Nonverbal Examples	Example and Message Sent Nonverbally
Facial Expressions	
Eyes	
Gestures	
Stance and Posture	
Touch	
Space	
Motion	
Time	

TASK 6.3   The Communication Process

Answer the following questions. Check your responses with those given at the end of the chapter.

1. As a teacher your major concern related to communication should be with the encoding and sending of information.   (True/False)

2. The two components of the spoken word are the

   _____ and the _____.

3. We tend to send various messages through the manner of our spoken word.   (True/False)

4. Define nonverbal communication.

   _____

   _____

5. Teachers sometimes communicate undesirable messages through their expressions and mannerisms.   (True/False)

6. Briefly describe five nonverbal languages that can be used to convey messages and information.

    a. _____

       _____

    b. _____

       _____

    c. _____

       _____

    d. _____

       _____

    e. _____

       _____

LISTENING

Listening is an art. We have all known someone in our life who, no matter what was being said, really listened. Real listening is hard work, harder than talking. The natural tendency of most people is to talk rather than listen. Although the art of listening takes effort and discipline, all teachers should develop and refine the skill since, once mastered, it pays handsome dividends both inside and outside the classroom.

The first step in learning to listen is to cut down on talking. Most of us have learned this to some extent. Although as children we tend to go on and on, oblivious to the reactions of those around us, we soon learn from adults that this is unacceptable behavior. But cutting down on talking is only the start of becoming a really active listener.

Listening is an active process that can be divided into three sequential steps. The three steps form a continuum with attention being the first phase, understanding the middle phase, and evaluation the final phase. The first step, attentiveness, is the key to the whole process.

The Attention Process

The attention process involves focusing on the speaker and the message being transmitted (Freedman, 1983, p. 5). To listen you must put on the "stops," that is, you must stop talking, stop fidgeting, stop letting your mind wander and "lock in" on what the speaker is saying. In short you must learn to block out everything else around you.

Blocking out is not an easy task and may not always be a desirable behavior for teachers who must be aware of everything that is happening in the classroom. However, as a teacher you must learn to pay strict attention to your students when the situation calls for it.

Attentiveness to a speaker is often related to the relevance of the message as well as to its intensity, concreteness, duration, and the setting in which it is delivered. In some cases you may not like what the speaker is saying or you may not see its importance, but you will never know unless you listen. You must sit it out. Often you will be unable to control all the variables that affect listening, but an awareness of the variables is a step toward controlling them.

The way one views a speaker also affects listening. If someone is described as being very intelligent or very important, we tend to listen more intently. This also applies to speakers who are attractive or who hold values, beliefs, and attitudes similar to our own. Other factors such as size, dress, and name may also affect our tendency to listen. All such variables must be controlled to the best of our ability in order to truly listen.

Listening, as well as talking, consists of both a verbal and nonverbal component. What reaches us through words is only one aspect of listening. We also gain information through nonverbal means, that is, through the interplay of gestures, feelings, body movements, and so on, which are always present when people interact. People sometimes believe they are sending a planned verbal message when their voice, choice of words, and gestures all indicate a completely different message.

Sokolove, Sadker, and Sadker (1986, p. 232) identify four nonverbal cues that affect communication. They suggest that communication and attentiveness can be improved by giving special attention to:

1. *Eye contact.* Focusing your eyes directly on the speaker shows interest. However, be careful that the direct eye-to-eye contact does not make the speaker uncomfortable.

2. *Facial expressions.* Your expressions show that you are really listening. Expressions give feedback (positive and negative) to the speaker as to whether the message is

being communicated. If not the speaker can make changes to assist you in your listening.

3. *Body posture.*   A relaxed listener is a better listener. It also tends to relax the speaker and stimulate further expression. A listener who is relaxed and leans toward the speaker communicates interest and involvement.

4. *Physical space.*   Move to a position that provides a comfortable space between you and the speaker. Avoid being too close or too far away.

Although much of the nonverbal information we receive is on a conscious level, much is also received at the subconscious level. For example you may dislike someone on sight for ''no reason at all.'' Or you may know that a friend has a problem even though there is no way you *could* know. This subconscious information plays an important role both in the decoding process and in forming an overall impression of the message. Sometimes we form inaccurate inferences about people based on subconscious information.

The Understanding Process

Understanding involves mentally processing the information received. In this phase the listener actively selects and organizes information based on judgments regarding its relevance and worthiness (Friedman, 1983, p. 5). You judge the information and decide, ''Am I really interested?'' The judgment is based on your perceptions of what is being said. But have you really understood? Listening is more than public relations, that is, pretending to understand. To really listen you must sometimes seek clarification, since true comprehension is always the ultimate goal.

The Evaluation Process

The last phase of the listening process is evaluation. In this phase one ''is weighing the message against beliefs, questioning the speaker's motives, challenging the ideas presented, suspecting the validity of the message, holding the speaker's ideas up to standards of excellence, wondering what has been omitted, thinking how the message could have been improved, and in other ways evaluating what is being said'' (Friedman, 1983, p. 5). Such evaluation is based upon the internal beliefs and values one holds. Thus, to really listen one must learn to evaluate information on its own merit. You must guard against modifying messages to better fit the beliefs and values you hold. This ability is difficult, and it takes self-discipline. However, it is well worth the effort, especially to teachers.

Effective listening then is more than just being silent. It requires comprehension, the ability to grasp the main ideas of what is heard. Active listening, like thinking, is an intense, dynamic process that involves "listening between the lines." You must adjust to the pace of the speaker and actively process what is being said. It takes concentration and discipline.

Past experiences and internal feelings often have an affect on what we hear. We all have emotional filters that may block certain words or phrases or, conversely, may allow others to rush in and overwhelm us. They may at times even change what we hear, as in the case of such loaded words as *lice, yankee, test,* or *radical.* Listening, like observing, is always selective to some degree. Task 6.4 should reveal some of your filters.

TASK 6.4   Identifying Personal Listening Filters

Write down all the things that have impaired your ability to listen at some time in your life, that is, record words or experiences that have made it difficult for you to receive and decode messages accurately. These filters can be physical, social, or emotional. Compare your list with others. Are the lists identical? Is your list composed of items in only one area?

Although the lists will vary among individuals, possible responses are found at the end of the chapter.

Nichols and Stevens (1957, pp. 102–3) offer three guidelines for reducing the effects of your listening filters. They include:

1. Withholding evaluation until the total message has been received. Again this requires self-discipline.

2. Hunting for negative evidence related to the message. Do not take what you hear at face value. Look for evidence that disputes what you hear.

3. Making a realistic self-analysis of what you hear. Test the message against your own biases, values, and feelings.

Nichols and Stevens also suggest that some people are poor listeners because they have developed bad listening habits. These bad habits include:

1. *Faking attention.*   One who is faking attention appears to be listening, but in reality is thinking about other things.

2. *"I-get-the-facts" listening.*   For some reason many people listen only for the facts in a message. However, memorizing

facts is not the way to really listen. An understanding of the main ideas that contain the facts is the most important component of listening.

3. *Avoiding difficult listening.* Some of us avoid listening when it takes mental exertion to understand what is being said. If you have such a habit, make special efforts to practice listening to difficult information.

4. *Premature dismissal of subject as uninteresting.* Some people automatically cease to listen when the message is of little interest. They equate interest with value. The fallacy in this habit is that the message is often worth hearing.

5. *Criticizing delivery and physical appearance.* This involves associating the importance of the message with the way it is delivered or the appearance of the speaker. However, it should be remembered that the content of most messages is more important than the method of delivery or the appearance of the speaker.

6. *Yielding easily to distraction.* You must learn to concentrate on the speaker and mentally shut out distractions to be a good listener.

In most cases an awareness of the preceding guidelines and pitfalls will automatically help you overcome their effects. However, you must actively practice the guidelines and avoid the bad habits if you want to become a really good listener.

Thinking can also affect listening. It is a well-established fact that listeners can process incoming information faster than speakers can deliver it. Consequently listeners often drift off on mental tangents that interrupt their listening. To be a good listener you must learn to keep your thought processes harnessed to what is being said.

REFLECTIVE LISTENING

Reflective listening is listening with feeling as well as with cognition. It is an earnest attempt to vicariously identify with the speaker's experiences and to respond to that experience. It calls for careful attention to both the verbal and nonverbal cues given by the speaker. The listener puts these cues together into a statement that reflects the full meaning of the speaker's message, both its content and associated feelings.

The response portion of reflective listening is an attempt to avoid misinterpreting the speaker's message or to further clarify it.

Sokolove, Sadker, and Sadker (1986, p. 230) note that a teacher's response in reflective listening involves holding up a mirror to the student's words, feelings, and behaviors. Thus, the teacher provides direct feedback regarding the success of the student's communications. This response can take the form of simple paraphrasing of the speaker's words or can be the listener's interpretation of the message as reflected in the verbal and nonverbal behaviors. For example your response to a student who tells you that he hates coming to school might be, "I believe you are saying that coming to school upsets you for some reason."

Listener responses can reflect either the content or the emotional components of the message. For example to reflect the content of a message, the listener might respond with a statement such as "Are you saying . . ?" or "I believe you are saying. . . ." To reflect the affective component of a message, one might respond with "I think you are feeling . . ." or "You appear to feel . . . ."

In summary the importance of good listening to the teaching-learning process is more recognized and accepted today than ever before. Listening skill is now viewed as being directly related to teacher effectiveness. All teachers need the skill.

Take a few minutes to complete Task 6.5, which will check your understanding of the listening process.

TASK 6.5   The Listening Process

Answer the following questions. Check your responses with those given at the end of the chapter.

1. All good talkers are good listeners.   (True/False)

2. Listening is an active process.   (True/False)

3. Listening is an easy task for most people since it requires only the use of the ears.   (True/False)

4. Briefly describe the three components of the listening process.

   a. _____

   _____

   b. _____

   _____

   c. _____

   _____

5. Reflective listening is concerned only with the affective component of a message.   (True/False)

FEEDBACK

The communication process requires that a specific message be encoded and transmitted by one person and received and accurately decoded by a second person. This is a continuous, two-way process in any interactive encounter. The listener is continuously decoding the information being sent and returning a message that is often nonverbal.

Listeners are continuously sending nonverbal messages of understanding or uncertainty, agreement or disagreement, liking or distaste, concern or lack of concern, attention or inattention. This feedback, when received by the speaker, should be used to modify or clarify the original message. Perceptive teachers respond to feedback from students by re-explaining, using further examples, or changing their mode of instruction.

Identifying and responding to feedback is a skill all teachers should learn. Task 6.6 gives you further practice at identifying feedback.

TASK 6.6 Identifying Feedback

Observe a discussion period in one of your courses or a conversation among several people. Note any nonverbal feedback sent from the listener to the speaker and note whether the speaker responds to the feedback. Record your observations. Possible observations and reactions can be found at the end of the chapter.

Nonverbal Feedback to Speaker	Speaker's Response to Feedback
1.	1.
2.	2.
3.	3.
4.	4.
5.	5.
6.	6.
7.	7.
8.	8.
9.	9.

Although responding to feedback in the learning environment is an effective way to improve instruction, many teachers rarely, if ever, use feedback as part of their teaching strategy. The most effective teachers know that feedback is too valuable to be avoided or ignored.

SUMMARY

Teachers communicate with students to bring about learning. Teacher interactions consist of both a spoken and nonverbal message with the spoken message having a verbal and vocal component. The verbal component is the actual words spoken, but the vocal component is the meaning attached to the words depending upon the voice loudness, pitch, inflection, tone, and rate.

Communication is central to the learning process. Without communication learning could not take place. Although most teachers understand the importance of verbal communication, many underestimate how much students learn from a teacher's facial language, body language, use of space and motion, use of time, and use of the voice.

Teachers and students should both acquire listening skills, since they are essential to both teaching and learning. It is impossible to learn without skill in listening. Also, better listening on a teacher's part will result in more effective teaching. Teachers must learn to control the bad habit of talking too much and actively listen. They must "listen between the lines," adjust to the pace of the speaker, and concentrate on the message sent. Moreover, teachers need to practice the art of reflective listening, that is, they must learn to listen with feeling as well as with cognition.

Teachers generally talk too much. They have not learned to use nonverbal communication effectively, and rarely, if at all, have they learned to really listen to students and to use the feedback students continuously send regarding lesson understanding. Since teachers fulfill their function through communication, it is essential that they develop an understanding of and skill in all facets of the communication process.

Answer Keys

TASK 6.1   Verbal Communication

Possible observations of differences between verbal messages and vocal messages include:

1. "I really enjoy my work." A monotone voice with no variation in pitch or tone conveys a neutral attitude or a dislike for work.

2. "He is such an interesting person." A voice with no variation or reflections could indicate dislike of the person.

3. "I'm not too excited about next week." A fast voice rate and higher pitch could indicate excitement about the next week.

4. "Good idea." Steady tone with no variation could indicate the idea was not so good.

5. "I wasn't a bit afraid!" Quiver to voice, fast rate, and high pitch would indicate fear.

Possible observations of vocal messages and voice qualities include:

1. *Excitement*   High voice tone, fast rate.

2. *Thinking*   Slow rate, hesitant with words.

3. *Happiness*   High voice tone, high pitch, fast rate.

4. *Interest*   High pitch, reflection at word endings.

5. *Anger*   Loud voice with high pitch, voice variation.

TASK 6.2   Nonverbal Communication

Observed nonverbal message possibilities include:

1. *Raised eyebrows*   Surprise at something being said

2. *Wink*   A joke on a group member

3. *Rigid posture*   Uncomfortable about something being discussed

4. *Looking at watch*   In a hurry to leave

5. *Backing away from individual*   Dislike of individual

6. *Fist hit into palm of other hand*   Stress a point

7. *Hard stare*   Disapproval

8. *Pat on back*   Doing something good

9. *Eyes looking away from speaker*   Not really interested in what is being said

10. *Continuous movement*   Restless

TASK 6.3   The Communication Process

1. *False*   You should also be concerned with receiving and decoding feedback.

2. Verbal component and vocal component.

3. *True*   The manner in which something is said will sometimes convey a message. Often this nonverbal message is more important than the verbal.

4. *Communications without words*   Communicating through the way we speak and use of bodies.

5. *True*   These messages are nonverbal in nature.

6. a. *Facial language*   The use of facial expressions that communicate.
   b. *Body language*   The use of the body and its parts to communicate
   c. *Space and motion language*   The use of space and movement in the environment to communicate
   d. *Time language*   The use of time to send information
   e. *Voice language*   Using voice intonation to communicate

TASK 6.4   Identifying Personal Listening Filters

Possible filters include:

1. Words such as: Republican, Democrat, hick, AIDS, Jew, communist, venereal disease, party, or school

2. Worry about someone

3. A special occasion

4. Just after an accident

5. An upcoming date

6. Past dislike for a subject or person

7. A fight with someone

8. A fight between parents

9. Hunger

10. An upcoming job interview

TASK 6.5   The Listening Process

1. *False*   Often people who talk too much are poor listeners.

2. *True*   Good listeners must think.

3. *False*   True listening requires one to think.

4. a. Attention to the speaker and the message
   b. Understanding, that is, selecting and organizing the information sent
   c. Evaluation, that is, judging the worth of the information against personal beliefs, values, and attitudes.

5. *False*   Reflective listening involves the content of the message and its associated feelings.

TASK 6.6　Identifying Feedback

Possible nonverbal feedback and responses include:

1. *Yawning*　Speaker speeded up presentation.

2. *Looking out the window*　Instructor moved to a new position and raised voice loudness.

3. *Reading book or newspaper*　Speaker paused, gave student a hard stare, and continued.

4. *Writing letter*　Instructor moved closer to individual.

5. *Talking*　Instructor stopped speaking.

ACTIVITIES

1. *Classroom observation*　Complete several observations in different level classrooms. Plan your visits to collect viable data related to the communication process. Collect observational data regarding:
   a. The effective use of verbal communications
   b. The different types of nonverbal communications used by the teachers
   c. The teachers' skill as effective listeners

2. *Listening in your present setting*　Using the Listening in Your Present Setting Worksheet that follows, record all that you hear in your present setting for five minutes. When finished compare what you heard with others in the same setting. Consider the following questions in your comparisons:
   a. Were the same things heard?
   b. Does past experience affect what is heard?
   c. Do internal feelings affect what is heard?

3. *Vocal communications*　Play a tape of an instructional episode with no video. List any information you note being sent through vocal communications.

4. *Nonverbal communications*　Play the tape in Activity 3 with video but no audio. List any information you see being sent by the teacher or the students through nonverbal communication.

LISTENING IN YOUR PRESENT SETTING WORKSHEET
(Five-Minute Time Limit)

Setting _____

Date _____   Time: from _____ to _____

Listener _____

List of what is heard

1. _____

2. _____

3. _____

4. _____

5. _____

6. _____

7. _____

8. _____

9. _____

10. _____

11. _____

12. _____

13. _____

14. _____

15. _____

16. _____

17. _____

18. _____

19. _____

20. _____

REFERENCES

Barbara, D. A. (1958). *The Art of Listening*. Springfield, Ill.: Charles C. Thomas.

Eisenberg, A. M., and Smith, Jr., R. R. (1971). *Nonverbal Communications*. Indianapolis, Ind.: Bobbs-Merrill.

Friedman, P. G. (1983). *Listening Processes: Attention, Understanding, Evaluation*. Washington, D.C.: National Education Association.

Galloway, C. (1976). *Silent Language in the Classroom*. Bloomington, Ind.: Phi Delta Kappa Educational Foundation, Fastback 86.

Hennings, D. G. (1975). *Mastering Classroom Communications—What Interaction Analysis Tells the Teacher*. Pacific Palisades, Calif.: Goodyear.

Hurt, H. T., Scott, M. D., and McCroskey, J. C. (1978). *Communications in the Classroom*. Menlo Park, Calif.: Addison-Wesley.

Miller, P. W. (1981). *Nonverbal Communications*. Washington, D.C.: National Educational Association.

Nichols, R. G., and Stevens, L. A. (1957). *Are You Listening?* New York: McGraw-Hill.

Sathre, F. S., Olson, R. W., and Whitney, C. I. (1977). *Let's Talk*, 2d ed. Dallas: Scott, Foresman.

Sokolove, S., Sadker, D., and Sadker, M. (1986). Interpersonal Communication Skills. In *Classroom Teaching Skills*, 3d ed, Cooper, J. M., et al. Lexington, Mass.: D. C. Heath.

Wolvin, A. D., and Cookley, C. G. (1979). *Listening Instruction*. Urbana, Ill.: ERIC Clearinghouse Reading and Communications Skills.

Stimulus Variation

After completing your study of Chapter 7, you should be able to:

1. Operationally define stimulus variation

2. Explain the purpose of stimulus variation

3. Identify and categorize six teacher behaviors that can be used to vary the stimuli in the teaching-learning environment

4. Explain the role of teacher enthusiasm in relation to stimulus variation

5. Explain the importance of avoiding distractors in the learning process

All of us seek stimulation. We are constantly looking for interesting things to do, for variety and challenge to enliven our daily existence. We prefer settings that provide stimuli rather than settings that are monotonous and dull. Stimulating environments arouse in us a state that is, within reasonable limits, a pleasant one. In short, doing something, no matter how trivial, is generally more interesting than doing nothing. Likewise we tend to prefer stimuli that are new, novel, or fast paced to that which is routine, familiar, and slow paced.

CLASSROOM STIMULATION

The human need for stimulation has important implications for the teaching-learning environment. The typical learning environment is under continuous bombardment from such external stimuli as street traffic, hall traffic, schoolyard activities, and weather conditions. All these stimuli interfere to some degree with the learning process and force the teacher to compete for students' attention. If external stimuli are more interesting or novel to students than the classroom learning activity, attention will more than likely be directed toward the external stimuli.

Students, especially younger children, have very short attention spans. If some new or changing stimulus does not occur in the learning environment after a certain period of time, they lose interest. Most of you have undoubtably had the same experience, for instance with an untrained speaker who stood rigidly behind a podium and put you to sleep with his or her monotonous voice. Unless you were extremely interested in the message, your attention soon turned to external stimuli or to your own inner thoughts.

Effective teachers consciously vary their behaviors and their learning activities so that students receive new or modified stimuli that keep their attention directed toward the learning process. These refocusing skills eventually become second nature to the experienced teacher. They become an essential part of the teacher's lessons.

Allen, Ryan, Bush, and Cooper (1969) suggest six simple behaviors or behavior patterns that can be used to vary the stimuli offered to students. These behaviors and patterns include the use of gestures, focusing attention, varying interaction styles, using pauses, shifting sensory channels, and using teacher movement.

Gestures

Gestures are effective attention-getting devices. In a crowd of people, your attention is usually directed to the person that is making some sort of gesture. The message received is that "This is where the action is.'' In classrooms a snap of the fingers or a nod of the head will focus student attention on you as you teach. Moreover, you can add emphasis through various general movements of the hands, head, and body.

You can effectively use gestures to refocus student attention or to emphasize a point in a lesson presentation. As students' attention wanders, a tap on the chalkboard or desk, a hand gesture, or a change in body position is often all that is needed to refocus attention on the lesson. These gestural movements represent a change in stimuli that usually results in directing student attention back to the teacher.

Focusing Attention

Focusing is probably the most common attention-getting technique used by teachers. Essentially it consists of directing students' attention to what you have said or will say through the use of either verbal statements or gestures.

Verbal focusing can be used to direct attention to certain specifics in a lesson or to redirect students' attention when it begins to wander. Refocusing students' attention is often necessary when the teacher has been speaking for a long time. Commonly used verbal focusing statements are, ''That was an important point, Mark,'' ''This is a major issue,'' ''Pay close attention to this point,'' ''This should be included in your notes,'' ''Know this diagram well,'' and ''That statement is important enough to be repeated.'' Learn to use such statements and gradually build your own personal repertoire.

Gestures are also effective at focusing attention. You are using this technique when you bang a desk, tap a map, use a pointer, use hand gestures, or make sudden movements with your body. The gestures represent new stimuli to students and will usually result in better attention.

An even better attention-focusing technique is to combine a verbal focusing statement with some form of gesture. Essentially the combination increases the intensity of the stimulus change. Examples of this technique include such combinations as:

[Teacher taps statement on chalkboard]: Remember this statement!

[Teacher slams one hand into the other]: This is a very important point!

[Teacher pats student on the back]: Great idea, Sam!

[Teacher simulates an explosion with hands]: An explosion can result if you aren't careful with these chemicals.

The imaginative use of such combinations can provide an effective stimuli change that results in increased attention and learning.

Varying Interaction Styles

There are four basic interaction styles that can be used in the average classroom: teacher-group, teacher-student, student-student, and student-group. You can use any one or a combination of these styles in the course of a lesson. The style or combination you choose depends to a large degree on the content and objectives of the lesson.

The teacher-group interaction style should be used when you want to address the class as a whole, as when you are giving a lecture or demonstration that covers new content. If questions are asked during the course of the lecture or demonstration, they are usually directed to the total group.

When you choose to address or question a specific student, the teacher-student interaction style is being used. This type of interaction is referred to as the Ping-Pong style since it usually goes teacher-student, teacher-student, teacher-student, and so on, with the teacher addressing or questioning different students in the group. Used wisely this style enhances student involvement in the lesson.

Under certain circumstances you may wish to redirect a student comment or question to another student for a response or for clarification. This is the student-student interaction style and is frequently used to acknowledge some student's accomplishment in the discussed area or to redirect an inattentive student back to the lesson. An example of student-student interaction is, "John, you did a report on France last week. Can you answer Mary's question?" Student-student interaction should be encouraged in class discussions since students often learn best from each other.

At times you may want to transfer the leadership of a lesson to one of your students. For example after redirecting a question or a request for clarification to one of your students, you might briefly withdraw from the discussion. This style should be used with care and only with students who can assume a central role in the group. Try to avoid putting your students in uncomfortable situations since some of them cannot take the pressure of leadership roles.

As Shostak (1982) suggests, you can often provide the stimulus necessary to maintain student attention simply through changes in the patterning of these interaction styles. For example you could intersperse a lecture with individual questions, have other students react to student comments, or withdraw almost entirely from a discussion by giving students leadership over the group discussion.

Using Pauses

As mentioned in the discussion of set induction, silence can be a powerful force. A sudden and unexpected silence can often put a stop to the most animated conversation. When background noise suddenly ceases, more than likely you are drawn to the silence and begin searching for cues that explain it.

This same principle can be used to focus or redirect student attention to a lesson presentation. This is particularly true when you have been speaking for an extended period of time and your words have lost their ability to stimulate the students. At such times appropriate pauses serve to refocus student attention to the message being communicated. In essence you deliberately reduce the stimuli in order to force students to strain for stimulus cues.

Many teachers appear to be afraid of silence and consequently do not use pauses. These teachers too often feel that for learning to take place there must be some form of continuous oral communication. They rush to fill in any silences that might occur. The result is often loss of student attention.

Teacher pauses can serve functions other than stimulus variation. Among the possible related uses suggested by Allen, Ryan, Bush, and Cooper (1969, p. 24) are:

1. To break the lesson content up into smaller units so that it is more easily understood by students

2. To serve as a cue to students to search for direction in the lesson

3. To prepare students for the next statement to be made by the teacher

As a teaching technique, pauses or silence has much to offer teachers. Contrasting sound with silence provides alternating stimuli to students and usually results in better attention and hopefully in more and better learning.

Shifting Sensory Channels

Although most communication in the average classroom revolves around teacher talk, there are four other sensory channels—seeing, touching, tasting, smelling—through which learning can take place. Consequently you can provide stimulus variation by shifting between these sensory channels. The shifts require that students make a corresponding shift in reception modes. This results in their refocusing attention toward your presentation.

The use of the overhead projector is a typical example of refocusing by shifting sensory channels. Students are required to shift their primary reception from aural to visual. To make the shift even more effective, you could ask that students acquire some information through visual means alone, that is, without any oral comment.

Tactile (touch), gustatory (taste), and olfactory (smell) senses can be used when appropriate learning materials are available. Sampling or manipulating such materials in conjunction with oral discussion requires refocusing attention on the lesson presentation.

Teacher Movement

Any physical movement by the teacher, who is normally the most significant person in the classroom, naturally draws students' attention. You can effectively refocus student attention by incorporating into your lesson simple movements that require some aural and visual adjustments on the part of students. The possible movements available to you are:

1. Moving to the left or the right
2. Moving to the back or the front
3. Moving among the students

Rather than remaining stationary (hiding) behind a podium or desk, teachers should activate the environment with their movement. Lateral movement is frequently used to draw attention to something in the environment or on the chalkboard. Movement to the back of the room or among the students allows the teacher to become less conspicuous and permits better student-student interaction.

Since student attention must be maintained for effective instruction, it is important that you develop skill in focusing it on the lesson presentation. To test your understanding of the stimulus variation techniques available to teachers, complete Task 7.1.

TASK 7.1   Identifying Stimulus Variation Techniques

Label the following stimulus variation techniques as examples of gestures (G), focusing attention (FA), varying interaction styles (VIS), using pauses (P), shifting sensory channels (SSC), or teacher movement (TM). Check your responses with those given at the end of the chapter.

_____   1.   "That's an interesting question, Jenny. Could you answer it Mark?"

_____ 2. As she lectures, Mrs. Jones slowly walks to the side of the room.

_____ 3. Mr. Franklin, the English teacher, simulates the action of the wind with his hands as he reads a poem entitled "The Wind."

_____ 4. Ms. Ferguson writes the new vocabulary words on the chalkboard as she speaks.

_____ 5. "Make special note of this issue! It was one of the most important of the Civil War."

_____ 6. The teacher pauses for a few seconds following a statement, then continues.

_____ 7. In the class discussion of other lands, Mrs. Smith shows the children pictures of the country being discussed.

_____ 8. "Who is the present secretary of state?"

_____ 9. The teacher uses a pointer to emphasize a statement in the textbook by tapping the book.

_____ 10. As he speaks, Mr. Emerson moves toward the back of the room where two students are talking.

Teacher focusing behaviors should be consciously practiced at every opportunity. Through conscious practice they will become a natural, continuous part of your teaching style.

TEACHER ENTHUSIASM

Enthusiasm is contagious. Teachers who are enthusiastic about teaching and about the subject they teach tend to keep students interested. If the teacher expresses a high level of interest and a sense of importance about a topic, students often become spellbound, anxious to find out what is so interesting.

Research reveals that enthusiastic teachers produce higher academic achievement (Silvernail, 1979, pp. 27–8). Moreover, this relationship between teacher enthusiasm and student achievement seems to be directly related to the age of the students. Brophy and Everston (1976, p. 106) suggest that teacher enthusiasm is less important with young children than it is with older children and adolescents.

In short, enthusiasm should not be overlooked as a form of stimulus variation. Enthusiastic teachers who are intensely interested in their subject matter not only keep students' attention as a result of their energy and excitement but often transfer their enthusiasm to their students.

DISTRACTORS

Although stimulus variation techniques are quite useful in maintaining student attention, these same techniques, if overused, can draw attention away from the learning situation. If overdone, students may become more interested in the novelty of your presentation than in its content. This is especially true when the lesson content is familiar, ordinary, or less than exciting.

The overuse of any behavior, even a desirable one, can result in focusing attention away from the learning situation. Such common occurrences as the continual use of "uh" or "okay," silence used too often, continually pacing around the room or tapping a pencil can detract from a lesson, as can an overly enthusiastic teacher. That is, hyperactive or excessively emotional teacher behavior results in focusing student attention on the behavior rather than the lesson. One of the skills associated with stimulus variation, then, is to monitor your own behaviors so that they do not interfere with the learning process. Task 7.2 checks your understanding of stimulus variation.

TASK 7.2 Stimulus Variation Concepts

Answer the following questions. Check your responses with those given at the end of the chapter.

1. Changes in stimuli should be avoided in most classrooms since they would detract student attention from the lesson.   (True/False)

2. List the six teacher behaviors or behavior patterns that can be used to vary stimuli to students.

   a. _____

   b. _____

   c. _____

   d. _____

   e. _____

   f. _____

3. Silence can be used effectively in the classroom to vary the stimuli to students.   (True/False)

4. Teachers should always remain stationary when presenting lessons so student concentration is not broken.   (True/False)

5. It is possible to be too enthusiastic in the classroom.   (True/False)

SUMMARY

Since student attention must be maintained for learning to take place, you must keep student attention directed toward the lesson. Various stimulus variation techniques that can be used to gain and maintain student attention include:

1. The use of gestures

2. Focusing attention

3. Varying interaction styles

4. The use of pauses

5. Shifting sensory channels

6. Teacher movement

Enthusiasm is contagious. Teacher enthusiasm is an effective attention getter and will often be transferred to students, resulting in better student attention.

Although the skillful use of stimulus variation techniques will increase student attention and thereby promote academic gains, care must be taken. If used in excess, these stimulus variation techniques can result in too much attention being directed toward the teacher and too little toward the lesson.

Answer Keys

TASK 7.1   Identifying Stimulus Variation Techniques

1. *VIS*   Teacher redirects question to another student.

2. *TM*   Movement occurs during lecture.

3. *G*   Teacher uses hand gestures.

4. *SSC*   Students must shift back and forth between aural and visual modes.

5. *FA*   Verbal statement is used to focus attention.

6. *P*   Pause is used to focus attention.

7. *SSC*   Children are required to use both aural and visual receptors.

8. *VIS*   Teacher directs question to entire group.

9. *G*   Gesture is used to emphasize a statement.

10. *TM*   Teacher uses movement to refocus attention and proximity as a control technique.

TASK 7.2   Stimulus Variation Concepts

1. *False*   Changes in stimuli can and should be used in the classroom to keep student attention.

2. a. Gestures
   b. Focusing behaviors
   c. Interaction styles
   d. Pauses
   e. Shifting sensory channels
   f. Teacher movement

3. *True*   Lack of conversation or noise can be used effectively to provide a change in classroom stimuli.

4. *False*   Teacher movement should be used to maintain student attention.

5. *True*   One can overuse any stimulus variation technique.

ACTIVITIES

1. *Classroom observation*   Complete several observations in different teaching-learning environments. Plan your visit to collect data related to stimulus variation and teacher enthusiasm. Collect observational data regarding:
   a. The use of stimulus variation
   b. The difference types of stimulus variation utilized by the teachers
   c. Examples of teacher enthusiasm.

2. *Micro-teaching*   Teach a 20-minute mini-lesson to a group of students or peers. Use as many stimulus variation techniques as you can. If possible, videotype the lesson.

3. *Micro-teaching analysis*   Study the videotape you made in Activity 2. List your stimulus variations and determine how proficiently you used them.

4. *Teacher enthusiasm*   List the characteristics of an enthusiastic teacher. Recall the general characteristics of past teachers you have had that were enthusiastic. When finished, compare your list of characteristics with others.

REFERENCES

Allen, D. W., Ryan, K. A., Bush, R. N., and Cooper, J. M. (1969) *Creating Student Involvement.* General Learning Corporation.

Brophy, J. E., and Evertston, C. M. (1976). *Learning From Teaching: A Developmental Perspective.* Boston: Allyn and Bacon.

Davis, O. L., Jr., Gregory, T. B., Kysilka, M. L., Morse, K. R., and Smoot, B. R. (1970). *Basic Teaching Tasks.* The Research and Development Center For Teacher Education, The University of Texas at Austin.

Shostak, R. (1982). Lesson presentation skills. In *Classroom Teaching Skills,* 2d ed., Cooper, J. M., et al. Lexington, Mass.: D. C. Heath.

Silvernail, D. L. (1979). *Teaching Styles as Related to Student Achievement.* Washington, D.C.: National Education Association.

Reinforcement

After completing your study of Chapter 8, you should be able to:

1. Differentiate between positive and negative reinforcement

2. Describe the different types of reinforcement that can be used in the classroom

3. Describe the characteristics and components of a reinforcement system

4. Describe the effects of different reinforcement schedules on the patterns of response

5. Explain procedures that can be used to identify effective classroom reinforcers

6. Differentiate between praise and encouragement and explain the effects of each

Actions that bring pleasure tend to be repeated. This is only human nature. When a student works to obtain something, that "something" (object, action, event, etc.) acts as a reinforcer for that student. However, what reinforces one student may not reinforce another. Remember that reinforcement always increases the strength of some behavior. For example students who repeatedly ask to stay in from recess are being reinforced in some way. It should be kept in mind that any repeated behavior, appropriate or inappropriate, is somehow being reinforced.

Reinforcement, or the rewarding of desired student behavior, is a long-recognized and essential skill for classroom teachers. Once learned and refined, it will make you much more effective in the classroom. Too often, however, teachers unconsciously overuse the same reinforcers which leads to a loss in their effectiveness. Moreover, teachers sometimes unwittingly reinforce undesirable student behaviors, making their teaching less effective.

POSITIVE VERSUS NEGATIVE REINFORCEMENT

Reinforcement in the classroom can occur in two different ways. **Positive reinforcement** occurs when teachers use a rewarding stimulus to motivate some action or behavior. The reward may be something tangible or intangible, such as grades, free time, praise, being named class leader, or being made to stand in the hall. Sometimes an event (made to stand in the hall) is a positive reinforcer for a student, even though it may not seem rewarding to the teacher. Many times positive reinforcement of inappropriate behavior occurs unintentionally in the classroom because teachers have a limited understanding of what students find rewarding. You should be conscious of this fact and try to diagnose the hidden reinforcers when an undesirable behavior persists.

Negative reinforcement involves removing students from an unpleasant stimulus, such as detention or the threat of punishment. Students are allowed to escape the unpleasant situation with appropriate behavior. Examples are sitting in their seat until they are ready to participate appropriately during an activity, staying in at recess until work is completed, or going to a time-out area until they are ready to settle down. Note that with the use of negative reinforcement, the student is in control. The negative situation can be escaped when the student chooses to perform the appropriate behaviors. Negative reinforcement is often confused with punishment, which gives the student no choice.

Positive or negative reinforcement is a powerful tool for motivating students and should result in an increase in some desired behavior. Moreover, when teacher reinforcement is withheld, undesirable behaviors will often desist. Now try your skill at identifying examples of positive and negative reinforcement by completing Task 8.1.

TASK 8.1   Positive and Negative Reinforcement

Identify the following as being an example of positive reinforcement (P) or negative reinforcement (N). Check your responses with those given at the end of the chapter.

_____   1.   "Steve, you can read your book when you finish the assignment."

_____   2.   "James, please sit down until you can behave appropriately."

_____   3.   "This paper is excellent, Jerry! You made some very valid points. Keep up the good work."

_____   4.   "Frank, go to the time-out area until you calm down!"

_____   5.   "Mary, since you raised your hand before talking, I want you to be class monitor next week."

TYPES OF REINFORCEMENT

Several types of reinforcement are typically used in the average classroom. The most effective type in any given situation depends on such variables as the grade level, individual student, learning activity, and teacher.

Verbal Reinforcement

Verbal reinforcement occurs when the teacher follows a student action or response with some type of positive comment. The most common verbal reinforcers are one-word comments or phrases such as "Good," "Excellent," "Correct," or "That's right." One should take care not to overuse these brief reinforcers or they will lose their effectiveness. Likewise, if *all* student comments are followed by verbal reinforcement, the comments will soon lose their effectiveness. Therefore, do not overuse verbal reinforcement and vary them so that they remain fresh and meaningful.

Another commonly overlooked form of verbal reinforcement is the use of student ideas. This technique can be used by applying, comparing, or building on contributions made by students during a lesson. Incorporating student ideas shows that what they say is important and usually increases the degree of student participation.

Nonverbal Reinforcement

Nonverbal reinforcement refers to the use of some physical action to send a message of approval for some student action or response. The physical action can be in the form of eye contact, a nod, a smile, movement toward the student, a relaxed body, or some positive gesture. Do not overlook the use of nonverbal reinforcement in the classroom; it may be even more powerful than verbal reinforcement. Research suggests that when verbal and nonverbal messages differ, students tend to respond to the nonverbal message.

Vicarious Reinforcement

People learn by observing others. If they observe others being reinforced for certain actions or behaviors, they tend to act in the same way if the reinforcement is desirable. This is termed **vicarious reinforcement**. For example if student A is praised for a certain action and student B desires the same teacher praise, student B will model the reinforced action. Such teacher statements as, "I like the way Mary raises her hand before talking," or "Mike's science report was excellent," or "Cindi always gets right to work on her assignments," are examples of the effective use of vicarious reinforcement. Vicarious reinforcement is usually more effective with younger students, however, it can also be used effectively with older students when the reinforcers are carefully chosen.

Vicarious reinforcement is usually efficient in that the desired behavior has already been modeled and consequently does not have to be taught. With properly chosen reinforcers and appropriate application, vicarious reinforcement can be used to teach new behaviors, encourage old behaviors, or strengthen or weaken inhibitions.

Delayed Reinforcement

Teachers usually reinforce students immediately following desired actions. However, it is also possible and sometimes desirable to reinforce students for some earlier action. For example a class question can be directed to a student who has shown prior knowledge in the subject area. This reinforcement of earlier action is referred to as **delayed reinforcement**. Through delayed reinforcement you show that actions or contributions are not forgotten but have continuing importance. It also reveals to students the importance you attach to earlier student actions.

Qualified Reinforcement

When student actions are only partially acceptable, you may want to reinforce the student in a manner that will motivate continued attempts at the desired action. In such situations you should use the technique of qualified reinforcement.

Qualified reinforcement occurs when you reinforce only the acceptable parts of a student action or the attempt itself. For example when a student gets a problem wrong at the chalkboard, you could reinforce the fact that the procedure used was correct, or you could reinforce the student's good effort. Or a student could be reinforced for presenting an interesting idea even though it was not related to the topic being discussed. Qualified reinforcement is an effective technique that can be used to get shy and less able students more involved in class discussions.

REINFORCEMENT SYSTEMS

You may sometimes want to use a more formal system of reinforcement. One program that has been highly successful is the **token reinforcement system** in which students earn tokens by performing teacher-desired actions or behaviors. These actions can be related to academics or to classroom behaviors. Tokens may be in the form of points, chips, holes punched in a card, stars, checks, play money, or anything else that seems appropriate. The tokens are then exchanged periodically for a reward. The reward can be such things as free time, less homework, food, tangible objects, being named class leader, games, free reading, or anything appropriate that is desired by the students.

One can also offer a menu of rewards in a token reinforcement system. Students then purchase the rewards for different numbers of tokens. It is usually wise to offer some less desirable rewards for only a few tokens and the most desirable rewards for a larger number of tokens. This way students will work for the higher number of tokens to get the more desirable rewards. For example with young children you might offer five minutes of free time for a few tokens and a little toy for several tokens. With older students you might offer being excused from a homework assignment for a few tokens and being allowed to listen to music in class for several tokens.

One advantage to using a formal reinforcement system is that no students are inadvertently overlooked and excluded from receiving reinforcement. In addition reinforcement systems have proven to be successful at both the elementary and secondary level, as well as in special classrooms.

The types of reinforcement used by a teacher depends on the situation. However, all types can be effective if used appropriately. Try your skill at categorizing the different types of reinforcement by completing Task 8.2

TASK 8.2 Identifying Reinforcement Types

Classify the following examples of reinforcement types as being verbal reinforcement (VR), nonverbal reinforcement (NR), vicarious reinforcement (VIR), delayed reinforcement (DR), qualified reinforcement (QR), or as an example of a reinforcement system (RS). Check your responses with those given at the end of the chapter.

_____ 1. "I like the way Susan got right to work on the assignment."

_____ 2. Kenny received three checks today for not talking out in class.

_____ 3. The teacher nods her head as a student talks.

_____ 4. "Excellent answer, John!"

_____ 5. The teacher makes good eye contact as a student answers a question.

_____ 6. "That's an important point Jane, but it doesn't really answer the question."

_____ 7. "I believe Helen can answer that question since she gave an excellent report on the topic last month."

_____ 8. "Mary's paper certainly is neat."

_____ 9. "That's a good point, Joe."

_____ 10. An hour of free time on Friday is earned if all homework is completed for the week.

_____ 11. "That's a good attempt at the problem, Edna, but the solution is incorrect."

_____ 12. The teacher writes a student response on the board.

_____ 13. "You're right, Alan, in that the disease is transmitted by an insect, but it isn't a fly."

_____ 14. "Good point, Mike. Elaborate on it."

_____ 15. "Sally, can you add to Ellen's point from your earlier study?"

If you had trouble with Task 8.2, reread this section on types of reinforcement, since it is an essential teaching skill.

REINFORCEMENT SCHEDULES

Timing and frequency of reinforcement are extremely important in reinforcement theory. Students are more likely to repeat an action if they are reinforced immediately after the action occurs. The longer you delay reinforcement following a desired student behavior, the less likely the student will repeat the behavior. Therefore, if a teacher wishes to encourage a certain student action, that action should be followed *immediately* by reinforcement.

Students learn faster when reinforced after each occurrence of a desired action. This is referred to as a **continuous reinforcement schedule**. Generally a continuous reinforcement schedule should be used in the early stages of learning. However, once the desired behavior has been established, it is best to use an **intermittent reinforcement schedule**, that is, to reinforce often but not following each occurrence of the desirable behavior.

An intermittent reinforcement schedule can be administered either on a ratio or an interval basis. If a student is reinforced only after a certain number of desired actions, a **ratio reinforcement schedule** is being used by the teacher. For example the teacher might praise a student after every third question is answered correctly. However, if the teacher praises a student after a certain amount of time, an **interval reinforcement schedule** is being used. Reinforcing students after every five minutes of time spent on their homework or in a cooperative learning situation would be examples of this method.

Ratio and interval reinforcement schedules can be further subclassified into fixed and variable schedules. A **fixed reinforcement schedule** is being used if the reinforcement is given after a fixed number of the desired behaviors (fixed ratio) or after a fixed amount of time (fixed interval). A fixed ratio schedule is being used when a teacher gives a student a gold star, say, after every fifth assignment is completed. However, if the student receives the gold star every second day for completing all the assignments, a fixed interval schedule is being used.

In a **variable reinforcement schedule**, no predetermined number of actions or length of time is used in administering the reinforcement. For example a variable ratio schedule is being used when a student is given praise for raising his or her hand before speaking after 3 times, then 10 times, then 5, 15, and so on. If the student receives the praise after 5 minutes, then 10 minutes, then 2, 15, and so on, a variable interval schedule is in operation.

Generally it takes longer to establish a desired action through intermittent reinforcement. However, one major advantage of intermittent reinforcement is that extinction is slower, slow **extinction** meaning that the desired action will continue without reinforcement for a longer period of time. Moreover, variable ratio and variable interval schedules are more resistant to extinction than are fixed ratio and fixed interval schedules because the students never know when reinforcement will come. The hope of reinforcement lasts longer when its application has been unpredictable. For example students working on a group project in the library or completing seatwork would be more inclined to stay on task when the teacher stops and checks their progress on an unpredictable basis. If teacher visits were predictable, students would be tempted to work only when the teacher is due. Since the ratio schedule is based on output while the interval schedule is more concerned with being on task, if you desire production, it is best to use fixed or variable ratio schedules. If your goal is to keep students on task, fixed or variable interval schedules usually work best.

Table 8.1 summarizes the different kinds of reinforcement schedules, as well as an example of each and their major advantage and disadvantage. An examination of the table suggests that, if possible, you should use a continuous reinforcement schedule in establishing a new desired behavior. This schedule generally works fastest. However, once the new behavior has been mastered, you should switch to an intermittent variable schedule of reinforcement since it resists extinction better once reinforcement is discontinued.

After studying Table 8.1 complete Task 8.3, which tests your understanding of the different reinforcement schedules.

TABLE 8.1 Reinforcement Schedules.

SCHEDULE	DEFINITION	ADVANTAGE	DISADVANTAGE
Continuous	Reinforce every correct behavior	Behavior rapidly established	Very rapid extinction
Intermittent Fixed Ratio	Reinforce after fixed number of correct behaviors	Slow extinction	Behavior established slowly
Fixed Interval	Reinforce after fixed time interval following correct behaviors	Slow extinction	Behavior established slowly
Variable Ratio	Reinforce after various numbers of correct behaviors (second, fifth, tenth, fourth, etc.)	Very slow extinction	Behavior established very slowly
Variable Interval	Reinforce after various time intervals following correct behaviors (5 min., 10 min., 8 min., etc.)	Very slow extinction	Behavior established very slowly

TASK 8.3   Reinforcement Schedules

Classify the following examples of reinforcement schedules as being continuous (C), fixed ratio (FR), fixed interval (FI), variable ratio (VR), or variable interval (VI). Check your responses with those given at the end of the chapter.

_____   1.   Ralph is praised every half-hour if he has stayed in his seat.

_____   2.   Liz is praised every time she raises her hand before speaking.

_____   3.   The class is occasionally given an hour of free time for being quiet when told to do so.

_____   4.   Joe is given a token for every fifth neat paper he hands in to the teacher.

_____   5.   Students in Ms. Smith's class are praised when they answer a question correctly.

_____   6.   At various times throughout the day, Mr. Harmon gives his students five minutes just to relax and talk.

_____   7.   Tammy is sometimes allowed to go to the library when her math assignments have been completed correctly.

_____   8.   Mr. Franklin allows his students time to discuss any topic they wish if there has been no class misbehavior for a week.

_____   9.   Students in Mrs. Anderson's class receive an extra point on their final grade for every two optional assignments they complete.

_____   10.   Mrs. Holt occasionally grades her students' progress on the term paper they have been assigned.

Because the effective use of reinforcement can greatly facilitate student learning, it is extremely important that you understand the different types of reinforcement and reinforcement schedules. Task 8.4 checks that understanding.

TASK 8.4   Reinforcement Concepts

Answer the following questions. Check your responses with those given at the end of the chapter.

1. Established behaviors usually result from some type of reward. (True/False)

2. Positive and negative reinforcement occur when a desirable stimulus is presented for an appropriate behavior.   (True/False)

3. List and briefly describe the five types of reinforcement.

   a. _____

   _____

   b. _____

   _____

   c. _____

   _____

   d. _____

   _____

   e. _____

   _____

4. A reinforcement system that uses tokens is most effective in the special education classroom.   (True/False)

5. Reinforcement should always immediately follow the desired student action.   (True/False)

6. An intermittent reinforcement schedule requires reinforcement after each occurrence of a desired behavior.   (True/False)

7. A fixed interval reinforcement schedule is being used when the student receives reinforcement once a week (Fridays) for appropriate behavior during the week.   (True/False)

8. A variable ratio reinforcement schedule is being used when the student receives reinforcement after 2 desirable actions, then 6 desirable actions, then 1, 4, 15, and so on.   (True/False)

9. Generally one should establish desirable behaviors through the use of intermittent reinforcement.   (True/False)

10. Extinction of desirable behaviors is slowest when a fixed schedule of reinforcement is used.   (True/False)

SELECTING REINFORCERS

Teachers must use care in selecting appropriate reinforcers for use with individual students. As noted earlier, what is viewed as a reinforcer by one student may not be a reinforcer for another. Thus, the best reinforcers for students are the ones selected by the students themselves.

There are various ways a teacher can identify student reinforcers, for example, through student observation, by simply asking the students, or through the use of student questionnaires.

Teacher attention is, for most students, an effective reinforcer. The attention can be either verbal or nonverbal, that is, it can be in the form of verbal statements or gestures that show you approve of the student's action. However, care must be taken in giving students attention. Remember that even criticism is a form of teacher attention, and some attention-hungry students will misbehave in order to receive negative attention.

A useful guide in choosing the most effective reinforcement is the **Premack principle**, which states that a preferred activity is an especially effective reinforcer for a less preferred activity (Premack, 1965). Simply stated the rule says: First do what I want you to do, then you can do what you want to do. Too often teachers reverse this procedure and allow students to do what they want with the promise that they will do what the teacher wants later. Of course they seldom get around to doing what the teacher wants. For example, visiting among students should not be allowed until seatwork has been completed. Do not accept the students' promise that they will do the work later.

Teachers use many different reinforcers in their daily interaction with students. They can grant privileges, give tangible rewards, grant free time, allow talking, grant exemption from assignments or tests, allow students to read magazines or play games, or simply give praise for a job well done. Whatever method is used to choose rewards for students, you must remember the importance of reinforcement and select reinforcers carefully.

MISUSE OF REINFORCEMENT

Reinforcement must be used with care, and it does not always bring about the desired learning or the desired student actions. Misused reinforcement can actually be detrimental to the learning process.

As mentioned earlier, one way teachers misuse reinforcement is to rely totally on one or two favorite types. These overused reinforcers soon lose their effectiveness. In fact, once students note their overuse and begin looking for them, these teacher behaviors can distract from the learning process. Perhaps the most commonly overused reinforcers are "Okay," and "All right." You should guard against their overuse.

Another way reinforcement can be misused is to reinforce virtually all student responses. Too often teachers feel that students should always be reinforced for their contributions, and thus, they reinforce students even when the response is not appropriate. Incorrect responses should *never* be reinforced, only the attempt or any part of the response that was on the right track (qualified reinforcement). A similar misuse occurs when a teacher reinforces unworthy responses or actions of their high-achievement students. Since these students are too often viewed as being superior, it is assumed that their responses *must* be superior and thus must warrant praise.

Given too quickly, reinforcement can detract from the learning process by blocking or interfering with the complete development of student ideas. One must take care that the student has finished before providing reinforcement for the ideas presented. Also, frequent reinforcement can interfere with student-to-student interactions by focusing attention back to the teacher with each new reinforcer. Thus, a two-way student-to-student interaction pattern can unwittingly be transformed into a three way student-teacher-student pattern. You must occasionally learn to wait before applying desired reinforcement. When all students have finished, you can then provide individual or group reinforcement.

Finally, some criticism has been voiced regarding the use of reinforcement. It is argued that its use weakens or slows the development of **intrinsic motivation** (motivation from within) and leads students to depend on **extrinsic motivation** (motivation from without). In other words, it teaches students to do things only for the external reward received rather than for internal satisfaction. However, if reinforcement is used appropriately and with care, this criticism can be avoided. Reinforcement should only be used with those students who need the extra incentive or when the desired behavior is unpopular or difficult. The reinforcement can then be phased out when it seems appropriate.

ENCOURAGEMENT

Teachers often use praise as a reinforcer in the classroom. However, one should use care in reinforcing with praise, because praise rewards the individual and tends to address the self-worth of the student. For example, praise statements such as, ''Good answer!'' or ''Good boy (or girl)!'' tend to convey the message that one is worthy only if the correct answer is known. This is not to say that praising a student's actions or responses should be avoided. We all like to receive praise at times, but we also like to receive encouragement. In fact sometimes we need encouragement to complete a task before we can receive praise for a job well done.

Encouragement differs from praise in that it stimulates the efforts and the capacity of the individual. Examples include, ''How nice that you figured that our yourself,'' ''Keep trying,'' ''Don't give up,'' ''I am sure you can solve the problem,'' ''I'm sure you can handle it,'' or ''You certainly are a hard worker!'' These responses encourage students to continue trying and not to give up.

Praise and encouragement are effective teaching tools when used with care. Teachers must know their students well enough so that they can praise or encourage them on an individual basis.

Take a few minutes to complete Task 8.5, which checks your understanding of selecting and using reinforcements.

TASK 8.5   Reinforcement Selection and Use

Answer the following questions. Check your responses with those given at the end of the chapter.

1. Describe three techniques you can use to identify student reinforcers.

   a. _____

   _____

   b. _____

   _____

   c. _____

   _____

2. Teacher attention can be used as an effective reinforcer.   (True/False)

3. State the Premack principle.

   _____

   _____

4. It is always good to use reinforcement in the classroom.   (True/False)

5. Praise and encouragement are basically the same thing, that is, they are reinforcers.   (True/False)

SUMMARY

Reinforcement is a much-used technique for stimulating students to respond in desired ways. Teachers can either apply a rewarding stimulus (positive reinforcement) or remove an unpleasant stimulus (negative reinforcement) to motivate students to some action or behavior. The nature of reinforcement is critical if it is to be successful. Reinforcement can be a verbal comment, a nonverbal action, a vicarious experience, a delayed comment, or a qualified comment. Select your reinforcers based upon the grade level, the individual student, and the learning activity.

Watch the scheduling of reinforcement. Use continuous reinforcement to establish desirable behaviors and switch to an intermittent schedule to maintain the behavior. An intermittent reinforcement schedule can be administered either on a ratio or an interval basis. When reinforcement is given after a certain number of actions, a ratio schedule (fixed or variable) is being used, whereas when reinforcement is given after a certain time interval, an interval schedule (fixed or variable) is being used.

There can be negative aspects to the use of reinforcement. You should avoid relying on a few favorite reinforcers, reinforcing all student responses, and giving reinforcement too quickly. Plan reinforcement well in order to encourage and maintain, rather than inhibit, desired actions.

Do not overuse praise as a reinforcer because it tends to reward the self-worth of the individual. Some students will benefit more from the use of encouragement, that is, from stimulation for the effort put forth.

Answer Keys

TASK 8.1   Positive and Negative Reinforcement

1. P	2. N	3. P	4. N	5. P

TASK 8.2   Identifying Reinforcement Types

1. VIR	2. RS	3. NR	4. VR	5. NR
6. QR	7. DR	8. VIR	9. VR	10. RS
11. QR	12. NR	13. QR	14. VR	15. DR

TASK 8.3   Reinforcement Schedules

1. FI	2. C	3. VR	4. FR	5. C
6. VI	7. VR	8. FI	9. FR	10. VI

TASK 8.4   Reinforcement Concepts

1. *True*   Almost all established behaviors are a result of some reward.

2. *False*   A positive stimuli is presented when using positive reinforcement, but negative reinforcement involves the removal of an undesirable stimuli following appropriate behavior.

3. a. *Verbal reinforcement*   A verbal comment of acceptance or satisfaction
   b. *Nonverbal reinforcement*   The use of a physical action to send a message of approval or satisfaction
   c. *Vicarious reinforcement*   Learning proper behaviors by seeing others being reinforced for those behaviors

    d. *Delayed reinforcement*   Reinforcing an earlier response or action

    e. *Qualified reinforcement*   Reinforcing only the correct portion of a response or action

4. *False*   Reinforcement systems can be effective in any classroom when used appropriately.

5. *True*   The longer one waits, the less effective the reinforcement.

6. *False*   An intermittent schedule requires that you reinforce often, but not following each occurrence of the desired action.

7. *True*   The time interval between reinforcements is fixed (constant).

8. *True*   The number of desirable actions between reinforcements is variable.

9. *False*   Desired behaviors are usually best established through the use of continuous reinforcement.

10. *False*   Extinction of desirable behaviors is slowest when a variable schedule is used.

TASK 8.5   Reinforcement Selection and Use

1. The responses will vary. However, possible responses are:

    a. Ask students what they want or will work for.

    b. Observe students during free time for ideas on what they like to do.

    c. Use a student questionnaire to elicit suggestions.

2. *True*   Teacher attention can be an effective reinforcer, but care must be taken not to reinforce negative behaviors.

3. First do what I want you to do, then you can do what you want to do.

4. *False*   The overuse of reinforcement can be detrimental to the learning process.

5. *False*   Praise is a reinforcer, whereas encouragement is a stimulator or motivator.

ACTIVITIES

1. *Classroom observation*   Complete several observations in different teaching-learning environments. Plan your visits to collect viable data related to reinforcement. Collect observational data regarding:

    a. The use of positive and negative reinforcement

    b. The different types of reinforcement used by teachers

    c. The different reinforcement schedules used in the learning environment.

    d. The use of praise and encouragement

2. *Micro-teaching*   Teach a 20-minute mini-lesson to a group of students or peers. Try to use as many of the different types of reinforcement as possible in your teaching. If possible, videotape the lesson.

3. *Micro-teaching analysis*   Study the videotape you made in Activity 2. Record your uses of reinforcement and reinforcement schedules. Draw conclusions regarding your use of positive and negative reinforcement, reinforcement types, and reinforcement schedules.

REFERENCES

Boules, A., ed. (1981). *Crossroads . . . A Handbook for Effective Classroom Management*. Oklahoma City, Okla.: Oklahoma State Department of Education.

Clifford, M. M. (1981). *Practicing Educational Psychology*. Boston: Houghton Mifflin.

Cooper, J. M., et al. (1986). *Classroom Teaching Skills,* 3d ed. Lexington, Mass.: D. C. Heath.

Premack, D. (1965). Reinforcement Theory. In *Nebraska Symposium on Motivation,* Vol. 13. Levine, D., ed., Lincoln, Neb.: University of Nebraska Press.

Wlodkowski, R. J. (1982). *Motivation*. National Education Association.

Woolfolk, A. E. (1987). *Educational Psychology for Teachers*. Englewood Cliffs, N.J.: Prentice Hall.

Questioning

After completing your study of Chapter 9, you should be able to:

1. Explain the importance of questioning to the teaching process
2. Explain the importance of using different levels of questions
3. Identify and differentiate between convergent and divergent questions
4. Identify and differentiate among factual, empirical, productive, and evaluative questions
5. Explain the importance of using different types of questions
6. Identify and differentiate among focusing, prompting, and probing questions
7. Define wait time 1, wait time 2, halting time, and silent time
8. Explain the importance of and benefits derived from the use of redirecting, wait time, halting time, silent time, and reinforcement
9. Identify guidelines that should be followed in effective questioning

Research indicates that in most classrooms someone is talking most of the time. Generally it is the teacher who talks and the students who listen. One way to switch from teacher-centered instruction to student-centered instruction is through the use of questions. Thus, skill in questioning becomes a vital component to effective teaching.

THE ART OF QUESTIONING

Questioning is basic to good communications. However, proper questioning is a sophisticated art, one at which few people are proficient despite having asked thousands of questions in their lifetimes. Questioning lies at the heart of good, interactive teaching. Questions must be at the appropriate level, be of the appropriate type, and above all, be worded properly. Moreover, the art of questioning requires that teachers master techniques for following-up on students' responses or lack of responses. We will now look at the different levels at which questions can be asked.

LEVELS OF QUESTIONS

Questions may be categorized as narrow or broad. Narrow questions usually require only factual recall or specific, correct answers. Broad questions, however, can seldom be answered with a single word and often do not have one correct answer. Broad questions usually require that students go beyond simple memory and use the thinking process to formulate answers. Although both kinds of questions are useful in the learning process, teachers traditionally rely too heavily on narrow questions at the expense of broader, thought-provoking ones.

Effective teachers adapt the level of questions to their teaching objectives. If learning specific information is the objective, then narrower questions are appropriate. If thinking processes are the objective, then broader questions are needed. Since thinking can take place at several levels of sophistication, it is important that teachers be able to classify and ask questions at these levels.

There are many classificational systems for describing the different levels of questions. Most of them are useful only to the extent that they provide a framework for formulating questions at the desired level within a classroom environment. Consequently some teachers may only want to use a two-level classificational system, while others may want to use a more detailed system.

One of the most extensive systems for classifying educational objectives (see Chapter 3 for a modified version) and classroom questions is that devised by Benjamin Bloom (1956). His system consists of six levels of cognitive thought, five of which can be further divided into sublevels so that it is possible to classify questions to an even greater degree. The six levels are:

1. Knowledge
2. Comprehension
3. Application
4. Analysis
5. Synthesis
6. Evaluation

Although Bloom's Taxonomy is extensive and very useful for classifying questions, most teachers find it too complex to use in the classroom. Instead of Bloom's Taxonomy, we will focus our attention on two alternative systems that will benefit you more. The first is the system of classifying questions as convergent or divergent; the second categorizes questions according to the mental operation involved in answering them. This second system was created by the author as a simplified version of the question types presented in Bloom's Taxonomy and is correlated with Guilford's Structure of the Intellect Model (Guilford, 1956).

The classification systems that are presented and discussed in this chapter are only two of the many systems that can be used effectively in the classroom. By using these or another system of questioning, you will significantly improve the quality of your questions and the quality of classroom interaction and learning.

Convergent and Divergent Questions

One of the simplest systems for classifying questions is to determine whether they are convergent or divergent. **Convergent questions** are those that allow for only one right response, whereas **divergent questions** allow for many right responses. Questions about concrete facts are convergent, while questions dealing with opinions, hypotheses, and evaluations are divergent.

Questions regarding concrete facts (who, what, when, and where questions) which have been learned and committed to memory are convergent. Examples are:

Who is president of the United States?

What is 5 + 3?

Where is Austria located?

What was the major cause of the Depression?

Convergent questions may also require students to recall and integrate or analyze information to provide *one expected* correct answer. The following questions are also convergent:

Based on our discussion, what was the major cause of the stock market crash of 1929?

Combining the formulas for a triangle and a rectangle, what would be the formula for finding the area of a parallelogram?

Based on our definition of war, can you name any countries that are now engaged in war?

Most alternate-response questions, such as yes/no and true/false, are also classified as convergent since student response is limited. Some examples of alternate-response questions are:

Is $x + y = 3$ a quadratic equation?

Is this a picture of a farm animal or a house pet?

Are the results what we expected from this experiment?

Is this logic statement true or false?

Is this statement an observation or an inference?

Conversely questions calling for opinions, hypotheses, or evaluations are divergent since there are many possible correct responses. Examples include:

Why do you suppose we entered World War I?

What would be a good name for this story?

Can you give me an example of the use of this word in a sentence?

Why is it important that we continue to explore space?

Who do you consider the greatest scientist that ever lived?

Divergent questions should be used frequently because they encourage broader responses and are, therefore, more likely to involve students in the learning process. They require that students think. However, convergent questions are equally important in that they deal with the background information needed to answer divergent questions. In the classroom it is generally desirable to start with convergent questions and move toward divergent questions.

In summary convergent questions limit student responses to only one correct answer, whereas divergent questions allow for many possible correct student responses. To check your ability to differentiate between and to write convergent and divergent questions, complete Tasks 9.1 and 9.2.

TASK 9.1   Convergent and Divergent Questions

Classify each of the following questions as convergent (C) or divergent (D). Check your responses with those given at the end of the chapter.

_____   1.   What can you tell me about Africa?

_____   2.   Which of these plants is tallest?

_____   3.   Mary, can you define a noun?

_____   4.   Do we have sufficient information to answer this question?

_____   5.   What do you suppose will happen to the lost dog?

_____   6.   What can we possibly make from these things?

_____   7.   What holiday do most people celebrate in November?

_____   8.   What would it be like to live in China?

_____   9.   Based on what you read in the textbook, what causes the different seasons of the year?

_____   10. Given a length of 15 centimeters and a width of 25 centimeters, what is the area of this rectangle?

TASK 9.2   Writing Convergent and Divergent Questions

Write two questions that are convergent and two that are divergent. You will not find an answer key for this task; you must decide by rereading the last section whether you have written acceptable questions.

1. Convergent

   _____

   _____

   _____

   _____

2. Divergent

   _____

   _____

   _____

   _____

Mental Operation Questions

In the late 1950s, J. P. Guilford (1956) published his Structure of Intellect, a model that classified all mental operations into five major groups: cognitive, memory, convergent thinking, divergent thinking, and evaluative thinking. Based on this model and the six levels of Bloom's Taxonomy, the Mental Operation System for classifying questions was developed. Table 9.1 shows the relationship between the Mental Operation System, Bloom's Taxonomy, and Guilford's Structure of the Intellect model. The Mental Operation System is basically a four-category system that combines four of Bloom's categories into two categories. In addition the system combines the cognitive and memory categories of the Guilford model into a single factual category. The four categories of questions that make up the Mental Operation model are factual, empirical, productive, and evaluative.

Factual questions test the student's memory. It is the simple recall of information through the mental processes of recognition and rote memory. Students simply recall information or recall and translate information. Factual questions are the narrowest of questions. Some examples include:

Who invented the automobile?

Nick, can you define the short story?

Mary, what did we do and see at the zoo yesterday?

Which side of the room is the longest?

What is the formula for the volume of a cone?

Empirical questions require that students integrate or analyze remembered or given information and supply a predictable answer. The question may call for a lot of thinking, but once thought out, the answer is usually a single, correct answer. That is, information

TABLE 9.1 Categories of Questions.

MENTAL OPERATION QUESTIONS	BLOOM'S TAXONOMY	GUILFORD'S STRUCTURE OF THE INTELLECT
1. Factual	Knowledge/comprehension	Cognitive/memory
2. Empirical	Application/analyisis	Convergent thinking
3. Productive	Synthesis	Divergent thinking
4. Evaluative	Evaluation	Evaluative thinking

must be applied correctly to arrive at a single answer, or the logical evidence of analysis must lead to a single valid conclusion. Empirical questions are also often narrow questions. Some examples are:

Based on our study of Germany, what conditions in that country led to World War II?

Given this triangle with a height of 4 centimeters and a base of 5 centimeters, what is its area?

What is the most economical source of energy?

Which of these two forms of government is the most democratic?

Note that these questions require that students recall learned information and use it to arrive at the correct answer to the question. However, there is only one correct answer.

Productive questions do not have a single correct answer. They are open-ended, and it is usually impossible to predict what the answer will be. They call for students to use their imagination, to think creatively, and to produce something unique. Productive questions are broad and require that students go beyond the simple recall of information. However, students need the basic related information in order to answer the question. Some examples are:

How can we improve our performance in mathematics?

What changes would we see in the attitude of society if we were to elect a woman president?

What are some possible solutions to the unemployment problem?

What do you suppose was the author's intent in writing this story?

Evaluative questions require that students make judgments or put a value on something. Like productive questions, they are often open-ended. However, they are often more difficult to answer than productive questions since they require the use of some internal or external criteria, that is, some criteria must be established for making the judgment. The responses to evaluative questions can often be confined to a limited number of choices. For example the question ''Which of these two paintings is better?'' limits the responses to two, whereas the question ''What is the best automobile made today?'' allows a number of responses. Other examples of evaluative questions include:

Who was our greatest president?

How would you rate our success in controlling hunger in this nation?

Do you think the author of the book developed the main character sufficiently?

Were the Indians treated fairly by the white man?

These questions require that students make a judgment based on some internal criteria. Therefore, it is often good practice to follow an evaluative question with an empirical or productive question asking for the reasons behind the stated judgment or value.

The Mental Operation System of classifying questions will give you the needed framework for improving your questioning skill. You should be asking questions at all levels of the system instead of at only the factual level, as many teachers tend to do. It is especially important that you ask more productive and evaluative questions than is common practice. These questions give students the opportunity to think.

Table 9.2 offers a review of the Mental Operation System for classifying questions. Study it carefully and complete Tasks 9.3 and 9.4 which will check your understanding of the system.

TABLE 9.2   Levels of Classroom Questions.

CATEGORY	TYPE OF THINKING	EXAMPLES
Factual	Student simply recalls information.	Define . . . Who was . . ? What did the text say . . ?
Empirical	Student integrates and analyzes given or recalled information.	Compare . . . Explain in your own words . . . Calculate the . . .
Productive	Student thinks creatively and imaginatively and produces something unique.	What will life be like . . ? What's a good name for . . ? How could we . . ?
Evaluative	Student makes judgments or expresses values.	Which painting is best? Why do you favor this . . ? Who is the best . . ?

TASK 9.3   Mental Operation Questions

Classify each of the following questions as factual (F), empirical (EM), productive (P), or evaluative (EV). Check your responses with those given at the end of the chapter.

_____   1.   Calculate the area of this circle.

_____   2.   What is your opinion of our court system?

_____   3.   According to the text, what was the main cause of the depression?

_____   4.   What do you predict will happen to the automobile in the next 20 years?

_____   5.   Who was the father of mathematics?

_____   6.   John, compare the work of Steinbeck with that of Hemingway.

_____   7.   How can we as a nation better meet the changing needs of our society?

_____   8.   Why do you favor the American form of government over the British form?

_____   9.   What does this story mean to you?

_____   10.   How do mammals differ from fish?

TASK 9.4   Writing Mental Operation Questions

Write two questions at each of the four levels of the Mental Operation System for classifying questions. No answer key is provided for this task; you must decide whether your questions are acceptable by studying Table 9.2 and rereading the last section.

1. Factual

_____

_____

_____

_____

2. Empirical

_____

_____

_____

_____

3. Productive

_____

_____

_____

_____

4. Evaluative

_____

_____

_____

_____

We have looked at two different systems for classifying questions. Either system can be used to improve your questioning skill. However, the Mental Operation System offers a greater degree of differentiation without the complexity attached to Bloom's Taxonomy. We will use this system in the remainder of this chapter.

TYPES OF QUESTIONS

Effective teachers must also ask the right type of questions, that is, you must adapt the type of question to your lesson objectives. For example you may want to ask questions to determine the level of your students' learning, to increase their involvement and interaction, to clarify understanding, or to stimulate their awareness. These purposes all call for different types of questions.

Focusing Questions

Focusing questions, which may be factual, empirical, productive, or evaluative, are used to focus student attention on the day's lesson or on material being discussed. They may be used to determine what students have learned, to motivate and arouse student interest at the start of or during the lesson, or to check understanding during or at the close of a lesson.

Did students read the assigned chapter? No use discussing the material if it was not read! Did the students learn and understand the material assigned? Can students apply the information? Focusing questions provide the answers to such questions. Factual questions can be used to check on basic knowledge at the beginning of or during a lesson. Empirical questions prompt students to figure out correct solutions to assigned problems and issues. Productive and evaluative questions motivate and stimulate student thinking and interest in a topic.

When asking a question to open a lesson or discussion, it is good practice to use a productive or evaluative question, since they tend to arouse students' interest and thinking. For example:

What do you suppose would happen if I were to combine these two solutions?

How could we test the hypothesis presented in the text?

Should the United States assume the role of world peace keeper?

Questions of this type should then be followed with questions at all levels to develop understanding and to maintain interest.

Prompting Questions

What do you do when a student fails to answer a question? Most teachers answer the question themselves or move on to another student. This tactic gets the question answered, but it fails to involve the original student in the discussion. It leaves that student with a sense of failure which, more than likely, will result in even less future participation. A better way to address an unanswered question is to use a prompting question as a follow-up.

Prompting questions use hints and clues to aid students in answering questions or to assist them in correcting an initial response. A prompting question is usually a rewording of the original question with clues or hints included. The following dialogue includes a prompting question:

"What is 5 plus 7 Pat?"
"I don't know."
"Well, let's see if we can figure it out. What is 5 plus 5?"
[Pause] "10."
Right, Now, we want 5 plus 7. How many more than 5 is 7?"
[Pause] "2."
"Good. So if 5 plus 5 is 10 and we add 2 more, what is 5 plus 7?"
[Pause] "12."
"Very good, Pat."

Note that in this example a series of questions is used to develop the prompting question: "So, if 5 plus 5 is 10 and we add 2 more, what is 5 plus 7?" This need not always be the case as we see next:

"What is the chemical formula for water, Henry?"
[Pause] "I don't know."
"Well, if a water molecule consists of two atoms of hydrogen and one atom of oxygen, what is its chemical formula?"
[Pause] "H_2O."
"Right."

Students often respond to questions incorrectly. As a teacher you cannot let incorrect answers pass. Of course you could give the correct answer or have another student give it. However, a better tactic is to have the student analyze his or her initial response for the error. The following sequence shows the use of prompting questions to correct an initial student response:

"Can you give me a noun, Randy?"
[Pause] "Run."
"Let's look at that answer. What is a noun?"
[Long pause] "A person, place, or thing."
"Is 'run' the name of a person, place, or thing?"
[Pause] "No."
"Good. Can you give us another example?"
"New York."
"Very good."

Note that in this example the teacher asks the student to examine the initial answer and then assists the student in arriving at a correct response through the use of prompting questions.

The use of prompting questions should give students a sense of success when they finally answer correctly. These successes should act as reinforcers to students which, hopefully, will result in even greater participation.

Probing Questions

Focusing questions are used to determine the level of learning and to increase student participation, whereas prompting questions are used when no response is forthcoming. Another situation arises when student responses lack depth. In such cases you should ask students to supply additional information through the use of probing questions.

Probing questions force the student to think more thoroughly about the initial response. They are used to develop clarification, develop critical awareness, or refocus a response.

You may want to probe for clarification. Students sometimes give answers that are only half-answers or that are not well thought out. These responses should be followed-up with probing questions to force the student to think more thoroughly and to firm up the response. Examples of such probing questions are:

What do you mean by that?

What do you mean by the term . . ?

Would you rephrase that?

Could you elaborate on that point?

Can you explain more fully?

You may sometimes want students to justify their answers, that is, to develop their critical awareness. This can be accomplished through the use of probing questions, as in the following examples:

What is your factual basis for this belief?

Why do you say that?

What are you assuming?

What are your reasons for that statement?

Are you sure there isn't more?

Finally, you may want to probe to refocus a correct or satisfactory response to a related issue. Examples of such questions are:

Let's look at this answer with respect to . . .

Can you relate this answer to . . ?

What implications does your answer have for . . ?

Apply your solution to . . .

Can you relate Mike's earlier answer to the issue . . ?

The different types of questions are invaluable teaching tools. They can increase student participation and involve students in their own learning. You should become proficient in their use. Task 9.5 will help you do that.

TASK 9.5   Identifying Types of Questions

Read the following anecdote and identify the teacher's questions as focusing (F), prompting (PT), or probing (PB). Check your responses with those given at the end of the chapter.

_____   1.   "We've been studying polygons this week, and I want to review what we've studied to this point. What is a polygon? [Pause] Sandy?"
"A closed figure with 3 or more sides."

_____ 2. "Good, Sandy. Can you name one way that we use polygons in everyday life? [Pause] Mike."
"Road signs have the shape of different polygons."

_____ 3. "Right. What do we call a four-sided figure? [Pause]
Helen?"
"A square."

_____ 4. "You're right in that a square has four sides, but there are
many figures with four sides. What do we call all four-
sided figures?"
[Pause] "A parallelogram."

_____ 5. "That's another example of a four-sided figure. Do you
remember what the prefix *quad* means?"
"Yes, four."

_____ 6. "So, a four-sided figure would be a quad . . ?"
"Quadrilateral!"

_____ 7. "Can you name the quadrilateral that has only two sides
parallel and no sides equal? Sam?"
[Long pause] "I don't know."

_____ 8. "Does this help?" [Teacher draws trapezoid on the board.]
"A trapezoid."

_____ 9. "Very good. Joe, name the triangle that has two sides of
equal length."
"Isosceles triangle."

_____ 10. "Okay. Do you see an example of an isosceles triangle in
this room, Mary?"
[Long pause] "Yes, the easel."

_____ 11. "Right. What is a regular polygon? Jan?"
"A polygon with all angles of equal size."

_____ 12. "Good. What else can you tell me about a regular
polygon?"
"All the sides are of equal length."

QUESTIONING TECHNIQUES

There are certain techniques associated with asking questions that
tend to increase the quantity and quality of the students' responses.
In this section we will look at four such techniques.

Redirecting

Redirecting is a technique in which you ask several students to
respond to some question, in light of the previous responses. It is
an effective way of building broader participation in classroom discussions. Since there must be several correct responses, the question

must be divergent, productive, or evaluative. The following is an example of how you might use the redirecting tactic.

"We have now studied the contributions of several great men and women of science. Which scientist do you think made the greatest contribution?" [Pause. Several hands go up.]
"Carol?"
"Albert Einstein."
"Mary?"
"Marie Curie."
"Mike, your opinion."
"Thomas Edison."

Notice that in using the redirecting tactic, you do not react to the student response. Your function is simply to redirect the question to another student. Thus student participation and involvement are increased, which should lead to greater learning and increased interest.

The redirecting technique can also be used effectively with students who do not volunteer to answer questions. It is important to involve nonvolunteers since, as noted earlier, participation leads to more learning and stimulates interest. The following is an example of how to use the redirecting technique to involve nonvolunteers:

"We've been discussing atomic energy as a source of power. However, there are dangers associated with its use. The question is should we develop it as a power source?" [Long pause. Several hands go up.] "Bob?"
"Yes, I think we should. We can build with a lot of safeguards."
"Okay. What do you think, Helen?"
[Long pause]: "I don't think we should. It's just too dangerous. We couldn't put in enough safeguards to make it really safe."
"Would you like to make a comment, Billy?"
[Long pause]: "I agree with Bob. I think we could make it safe to use."

It is important to note that, in this last example, the nonvolunteers are not forced to answer. Rather they are given the opportunity to make a contribution to the discussion. In addition note that they are given time to consider a response. This time is referred to as wait time, which we will discuss next.

Wait Time

Students need time to think, time to ponder the responses they will give to your questions. However, research (Rowe, 1974a, 1974b, 1978) has shown that teachers on the average wait only about *one* second for students to answer questions. Further research by Rowe revealed that when teachers learn to increase from three to five seconds the time they wait following a question, the following things occur:

1. The length of student responses increased
2. Failure to respond decreased
3. Questions from students increased
4. Unsolicited responses increased
5. Confidence of students increased
6. Speculative thinking increased

There are two types of wait time. **Wait time 1** is the initial time provided for the first student response to a question. **Wait time 2** is the total time a teacher waits for all students to respond to the same question or for students to respond to each other's response to a question. Wait time 2 may involve several minutes. If you wish to raise student involvement, you must learn to increase your wait time tolerance so that students have more opportunities to think about their answers.

The pattern of questioning that is all too typical in the average classroom is:

It is nothing more than a question-and-answer period. The teacher asks a question of an individual student, receives an answer, moves to the next student, asks a question, receives an answer, moves to the next student, and so on. Students are often given little time to think and express themselves and no time to react to each others' comments. In fact most of the questions are typically at the factual level. Appropriate use of high-level questions and wait time can often change this sequence to:

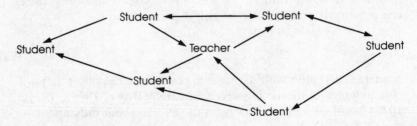

Rather than a question-and-answer session, you have a real discussion. Students give extended responses, comment on other students' responses, and ask questions. There is real interest and involvement. Thus, extending the time you wait following a question to three to five seconds and giving students time to react to other students' responses is well worth the added effort.

Halting Time

Halting time is similar to wait time in that you pause during what you are saying to give students time to think. However, no questions are asked, and no student comments are elicited. It is particularly useful when presenting complex material or directions.

In using halting time, you would present some of the complex material or directions and then stop so students have time to think or carry out the directions. While stopping, you would visually check with the class to see whether they appear to understand what you are trying to communicate. If the students do appear to understand, you continue. If on the other hand students appear to be confused, you may want to ask questions or redo the explanation or directions.

Listening

Learn to listen to your students. Listen to what they have to say, and when they have finished, and only then, formulate further questions or comment on their answers. Too often teachers are busy focusing on themselves while students are speaking. They are busy formulating the next question, the next explanation, or the next activity. In fact teachers are often so eager to continue that they interrupt or cut off students before they have finished.

Develop the use of silent time. **Silent time** is the time taken after a student has finished speaking and before you reply or continue. Research indicates that teachers wait on the average of only about one second following a student response. As with questioning, silent time should be increased to from three to five seconds to prevent you from cutting off students and to allow time for other students to interject their comments.

Reinforcement

Once you have asked a question and an acceptable response has been given, you must decide how to react. Should you offer praise or approval, or should you merely accept the response without comment and continue with the lesson? How you react, that is, your pattern of reinforcement, has a powerful effect on the direction of the interaction in the classroom.

Rewards and praise following student responses to a teacher's questions are effective in encouraging students to participate. Words like "good," "great," "What an outstanding idea," "super," and so on may be used to effectively reward a student's correct answer. A detailed discussion of reinforcement techniques was given in Chapter 8. You may want to review these techniques at this point.

Although some reinforcement is good, the too frequent application of reinforcement negates the benefits derived from wait time. Wait time is used to give students time to think and to give other students the opportunity to respond. However, if you reinforce students early in an answering sequence, other students may decide not to respond because they fear their answer could not be as good as the earlier response. After all, you did say the earlier response was "super."

Rather than giving reinforcement after the initial response to a question, you should allow as many students as possible to respond, then reinforce all of them for their contributions. You can return to the best answer for further comment.

This concludes our discussion of various techniques that can be used to improve one's skill at questioning. The next section gives some general guidelines on questioning. Before we continue, however, let us focus on two tasks involving questioning techniques.

TASK 9.6   Questioning Technique Definitions

Label the following definitions as wait time 1 (W1), wait time 2 (W2), halting time (HT), or silent time (ST). Check your responses with those given at the end of the chapter.

_____   1.   The time you wait following a student response before you continue.

_____   2.   The time you allow all students in class to respond to a question.

_____   3.   A pause used to give students time to think and ponder.

_____   4.   The time you wait for the initial response to a question.

TASK 9.7   Questioning Technique Summary

Answer each of the following regarding the use of various questioning techniques. Check your responses with those given at the end of the chapter.

1.   The appropriate use of wait times will usually lead to greater student participation.   (True/False)

2. Student question responses should always be reinforced.   (True/False)

3. The redirecting tactic requires that a student respond to a question in light of another student's response.   (True/False)

4. Teacher silent time should be about one second.   (True/False)

5. The use of halting time requires that you be proficient at asking higher-level questions.   (True/False)

6. Wait time 1 may be as long as several minutes.   (True/False)

7. The redirecting tactic may be used successfully with nonvolunteers. (True/False)

QUESTIONING GUIDELINES

Asking good questions is an art that can be mastered with practice. The following guidelines will be helpful as you refine your skill at questioning.

1. *Ask clear questions.*   Questions should ask something definite in simple, clear, straightforward language that students can understand. Avoid ambiguous, confusing constructions, and excess verbiage.

2. *Ask your question before designating a respondent.*   Ask the question, wait for the class to think about it, and then ask someone for an answer. As usual, there are exceptions to this rule. When you call on an inattentive student, it is often better to call the name first so that the question is heard. Similarly you should call the name first when addressing slow or shy students so that they can prepare themselves.

3. *Ask questions that match your lesson objectives.*   When facts are wanted, ask factual and empirical questions. When you want to stimulate student thinking, ask productive and evaluative questions. Use the different levels of questions.

4. *Distribute questions about the class fairly.*   Avoid directing all questions to a few, bright students. However, also avoid some mechanical system for asking questions. Students soon catch on to such systems as going by alphabetical order or going row by row and will only pay attention when they know it is their turn.

5. *Ask questions suited to all ability levels in the class.*   Some questions should be easy and some difficult so that all students have a chance to respond to some questions correctly.

6. *Ask only one question at a time.*   Asking two or three questions at once often confuses students. Multiple questions permit no time to think and, since several questions were asked, students are not sure which question to answer first.

7. *Avoid too many questions.*   It is usually much more effective to establish a knowledge base before initiating a questioning sequence. This is especially true when higher-level questions are to be asked.

8. *Pause for at least three seconds following each question.*   A three-second pause gives students time to think and to formulate their answers.

9. *Use questions to help students modify their responses.*   Use prompting and probing questions to help students more thoroughly think about their responses. This keeps students involved in the lesson, develops better thinking skills, and reinforces the fact that students can be successful.

10. *Avoid too many questions that give away answers and one-word-answer questions.*   These questions do nothing to stimulate student thinking and, when used too often, lead to boredom.

11. *Reinforce student answers sparingly.*   Remember that the reinforcement of every student response can kill a discussion. Students often fear they will be unable to compete against the preceding reinforced responses.

12. *Listen carefully to student responses.*   Wait at least three seconds following an answer to give the student time to make further comments and to allow other students time to react to the first response.

SUMMARY

Asking good questions involves more than simply asking students clear questions regarding specific content. You must adapt questions to your lesson objectives. The questions may be categorized as narrow or broad. Factual recall of information requires the use of narrow questions (convergent), whereas the desire to stimulate thinking calls for the use of broad questions (divergent).

A more detailed system for classifying questions is sometimes needed. Is the purpose of the question to determine whether the student holds certain knowledge or whether the student can use and apply the information? Such varied purposes require different levels of questions, from simple factual, to empirical, to productive, to evaluative. In addition your purpose requires that you ask the right types of question. Is your purpose to arouse interest and increase involvement? These purposes require the effective use of focusing, prompting, and probing questions.

Redirecting your questions, using wait time and halting time, listening well, and using reinforcement will enhance your skill as a questioner. These techniques widen student participation and improve the quality of student responses.

There is no end to the degree of sophistication your questioning skill may attain. Your task as a teacher is to practice and modify your questioning behavior in order to improve student learning and the social-emotional climate of your classroom.

Answer Keys

TASK 9.1   Convergent and Divergent Questions

1. D   Many responses possible
2. C   Limited predictable responses possible
3. C   Only one correct response possible
4. C   Yes or no response
5. D   Many responses possible
6. D   Many responses possible
7. C   Limited predictable responses possible
8. D   Many responses possible
9. C   Limited to information from the textbook
10. C   Only one correct response possible

TASK 9.3   Mental Operation Questions

1. EM   One correct response
2. EV   Judgment required
3. F   Recall of textbook information
4. P   Many possible correct, unpredictable responses
5. F   Simple recall of information
6. EM   An analysis of recalled information required
7. P   Many possible correct, unpredictable responses
8. EV   Values expressed
9. P   Many possible correct, unpredictable responses
10. EM   Analysis of recalled information required

TASK 9.5   Identifying Types of Questions

1. *F*   Used to see if student has learned material
2. *F*   Used to stimulate thinking
3. *F*   Used to see if student has learned material
4. *PT* Hint given to correct response
5. *PT* Clue given to correct response
6. *PT* Clue given to assist student
7. *F*   Used to see if student has learned material
8. *PT* Clue given to help student arrive at correct answer
9. *F*   Used to see if student has learned material
10. *F* Used to see whether student can apply the concept
11. *F* Used to see if student has learned materials
12. *PB* Probe for additional information

TASK 9.6   Questioning Technique Definitions

1. ST   2. W2   3. HT   4. W1

TASK 9.7   Questioning Technique Summary

1. *True*   The appropriate use of wait times 1 and 2 have been shown to lead to greater student participation.

2. *False* Although the use of reinforcement may increase student involvement, overuse may be detrimental to student interaction.

3. *True*   This is the basic purpose of the redirecting tactic.

4. *False* Silent time should be from three to five seconds.

5. *False* No questions should be asked during halting time.

6. *False* Wait time 1 should be from three to five seconds.

7. *True*   The use of the redirecting tactic with nonvolunteers may get them involved in the lesson

ACTIVITIES

1. *Classroom question analysis* Construct an instrument to ana-
    lyze questioning in an observational setting. Use your con-
    structed instrument in several observational settings and
    analyze the results. Consider the following in your instru-
    ment construction and analyses:
    a.   What levels of questions are used most often?
    b.   Are questions clear?
    c.   Is time used effectively?
    d.   Is reinforcement used effectively?
    e.   Are various types of questions used?

2. *Micro-teaching* Teach a 20-minute mini-lesson to a group of
    students or peers. Try to use different levels of questions,
    different types of questions, and the various techniques dis-
    cussed in Chapter 9. Record the lesson.

3. *Micro-teaching analysis* Study the recording of your mini-
    teaching experience made in Activity 2. Use the instrument
    you constructed in Activity 1 to analyze the experience.
    What conclusions can you draw regarding your questioning
    proficiency?

4. *Investigating testbook questions* Obtain the teacher's and stu-
    dent's editions of a textbook for any grade level and subject.
    Choose one unit within that textbook and analyze the ques-
    tions contained in the student text and the questions sug-
    gested by the teacher's edition. What levels of questions are
    most frequently used?

REFERENCES

Allen, D. W., Ryan, K. A., Bush, R. N., and Cooper, J. M. (1969). *Questioning Skills*. General Learning Corporation.

Bloom, B. S., ed., Engelhart, M. D., Furst, E. J., Hill, W. H., and Frathwohl, D. R. (1965). *Taxonomy of Educational Objectives, Handbook I: Cognitive Domain*. New York: David McKay.

Davis, Jr., O. L., Gregory, T. B., Kysilka, M. L., Morse, K. R., and Smoot, B. R. (1970). *Basic Teaching Tasks*. The University of Texas at Austin.

Dillon, J. T. (1983). *Teaching and the Art of Questioning*. Bloomington, Ind.: Phi Delta Kappa Educational Foundation.

Falkor, L., and Moss, J. (November 1984). When teachers tackle thinking skills. *Education Leadership*, 4–9.

Gall, M. (November 1984). Synthesis of research on teachers' questions. *Educational Leadership*, 40–7.

Griffin, R. D. (January 1970). Questions that teach: How to frame them. How to ask them. *Grade Teacher*, 58–61.

Guilford, J. P. (July 1956). The structure of intellect. *Psychological Bulletin*, 53, 267–93.

Hyman, R. T. (1979). *Strategic Questioning*. Englewood Cliffs, N.J.: Prentice-Hall.

Rowe, M. B. (1974a). Wait time and rewards as instructional variables, their influence on language, logic, and fate control: Part one, wait time. *Journal of Research in Science Teaching*, 11, 2, 81–94.

Rowe, M. B. (1974b). Relation of wait time and rewards to the development of language, logic, and fate control: Part two, rewards. *Journal of Research in Science Teaching*, 11, 4, 291–308.

Rowe, M. B. (1978). *Teaching Science as Continuous Inquiry*. New York: McGraw Hill.

Sadker, M., and Sadker, D. (1982). Questioning skills. In *Classroom Teaching Skills*, 3d ed., Cooper, J. M., et al. Lexington, Mass.: D. C. Heath.

Sanders, N. M. (1966). *Classroom Questions: What Kinds?* New York: Harper and Row.

Wilen, W. W. (1982). *Questioning Skills for Teachers*. Washington, D.C.: National Education Association.

_____ chapter ten

Classroom
Management

After completing your study of Chapter 10, you should be able to:

1. Define classroom management and differentiate between discipline and punishment

2. Describe the three facets of classroom management

3. Differentiate between the authoritarian, democratic, and laissez-faire approach to leadership

4. Identify and discuss factors that influence the general atmosphere of a classroom

5. Identify various techniques that may be used to effectively motivate students

6. Identify and describe the general characteristics of the different models of discipline

7. Discuss control techniques that are commonly used by effective classroom managers

8. Identify and discuss various teacher-tested guidelines for effective classroom management

This is a book about teaching, but effective teaching requires that you also be an effective manager. Are you able to get students' co-operation, maintain their involvement in instructional tasks, and carry out the business of the classroom smoothly? If so, you are an effective manager. Many teachers have trouble with this aspect of teaching, essential as it is.

Central to effective management is classroom leadership and the ability to establish a classroom atmosphere that is conducive to learning. As an effective leader, you must be concerned with your ability to provide a positive social, physical, and intellectual environment which, in turn, requires that you possess the ability to communicate effectively and to motivate students.

Another highly important aspect of classroom management is the matter of discipline, which perenially appears as a major concern on surveys of teachers, parents, and administrators. Discipline should not be equated with punishment. Whereas punishment is the reaction to disruptive behavior, discipline is concerned with the prevention of disruptive behavior as well as reactions to it. Therefore, discipline is concerned with what you do to prevent behavior problems as well as what you do when problems occur. As a teacher, you should be skilled in both the prevention and reaction aspects of discipline.

Classroom management then consists of three major components: leadership, classroom atmosphere, and discipline. We will look at each of these in the following sections.

TEACHER TYPES

What type of person are you? Are you stimulating, warm, caring, fair, funny, and interesting; are you commanding, dominating, sharp, critical, and harsh; or are you lackadaisical and permissive? Personal characteristics such as these influence your leadership style, that is, whether you are inclined to be an authoritarian, democratic, or laissez-faire leader. Your leadership style will also be heavily influenced by such factors as the subject and grade you teach, the policies of the school, and the abilities of your students. Some students lack the maturity and ability to be involved in classroom decision making, and some school districts actively discourage such student involvement. Also, always keep in mind that you may, and should, change leadership styles as the situation warrants.

Authoritarian Leadership

Power, domination, pressure, and criticism is the authoritarian leadership approach. The teacher uses pressure and punishment to demand cooperation. The teacher assumes the sole responsibility of making all decisions for the class. His or her role is to control student behavior and to force compliance with a sharp voice and the use of fear. The authoritarian approach seeks compliance through the use of forceful external controls.

The authoritarian teacher uses criticism and "put downs" when students make mistakes. Research (Schmuck and Schmuch, 1971, p. 26) suggests that this style of leadership often results in an atmosphere of hostility, a feeling of powerlessness, competitiveness, high dependency, and alienation from the subject matter. Students in an authoritarian atmosphere often fear to take chances and often develop low self-esteem and a defeatist attitude. The students tend to give up when faced with a new or difficult task.

Democratic Leadership

The sharing of responsibility is the democratic approach to leadership. The democratic leader seeks compliance through encouragement rather than demands. The teacher is kind, caring, and warm, but also firm. Order is maintained by letting students participate as much as possible in decision making. Responsibility is taught on a firsthand basis by *giving* students responsibility. The democratic leader seeks to motivate through both internal and external means.

The democratic leader avoids criticism and "put downs." Instead, self-esteem is developed by sharing responsibility. Students are encouraged when they make mistakes, they develop a sense of belief in themselves. As a result, the classroom atmosphere is one of openness, friendly communications, and independence. Research has shown that productivity and performance are high in well-run, democratic classrooms.

Laissez-Faire Leadership

In a laissez-faire approach, the teacher is completely permissive. Anything goes! Everyone does his or her own thing. This style of leadership most often leads to chaos. It produces disorganization, causes student frustration, and results in little if any work. In addition, students often experience stress and a feeling of being totally overwhelmed and lost.

Many classroom problems can be overcome if we turn from the obsolete authoritarian approach of demanding obedience and turn to a more democratic approach based on freedom, choice, and responsibility. However, freedom does not mean that anything goes or that you abdicate your role as a leader. It means freedom with limits. Students need limits and guidance to become responsible individuals. The amount of freedom and the limits you impose will ultimately depend upon factors mentioned earlier: subject and grade, student abilities, and school policies. Generally younger children need more guidance and limits than older students.

Table 10.1 compares the characteristics of the different leadership styles. Study it and then complete Task 10.1, which tests your ability to differentiate between the three approaches to leadership.

TABLE 10.1 Characteristics of the Different Leadership Styles.

AUTHORITARIAN	DEMOCRATIC	LAISSEZ-FAIRE
Punishing	Friendly	Permissive
Faultfinding	Firm	Total freedom
Demanding	Encouraging	Anarchy
Commanding	Stimulating	Disorder
Critical	Helping	
Pressuring	Guiding	
Sharp voiced	Winning	
Imposing	Warm	
Dominating	Caring	
Harsh	Fair	
Fearful	Influencing	

TASK 10.1 Identifying Leadership Styles

Label each of the following as characteristics of the authoritarian leadership approach (A), the democratic leadership approach (D), or the laissez-faire leadership approach (L). Check your responses with those given at the end of the chapter.

_____ 1. Responsibilities are shared in the classroom.
_____ 2. The teacher decides, and students obey without question.
_____ 3. The teacher demands cooperation.
_____ 4. The teacher acknowledges and encourages achievement.
_____ 5. The teacher is firm and sets limits but is warm and fair.
_____ 6. There is freedom with few, if any, constraints.

CLASSROOM ATMOSPHERE

Your leadership style affects the general atmosphere of your classroom. However, other factors such as the physical environment, room arrangement, teacher motivation, and classroom communications also influence student behavior and general classroom atmosphere.

Physical Environment

An attractive room is conducive to learning. As a teacher you will in most cases have full responsibility for the appearance and comfort of your room. Will your room be attractive and colorful, or will it be bleak and drab?

Although most schools have custodians, during school hours it is your responsibility to keep a clean and neat room. Share this responsibility with students and make sure that places and procedures are designated for storing supplies, handing in papers, and disposing of trash. This kind of planning greatly enhances classroom functioning and helps maintain a pleasant, productive working atmosphere.

Ventilation, temperature, and lighting of the classroom also affect student comfort and ability to concentrate. A room that is too stuffy, too hot, too cold, or a room that has dim or bright lighting is often distracting, causing students to focus on their discomfort rather than on their work. It is your responsibility to see that these factors are properly adjusted or to see that they are adjusted by the proper person.

Bulletin boards and displays can add much to the attractiveness and atmosphere of a classroom. They should be designed to be both informative and colorful, and when student work is prominently displayed, they can be quite motivating. Having students design and construct classroom bulletin boards and displays gives added meaning to the classroom environment. It becomes their room, a place to be proud of and to be cared for.

Room Arrangement

Classroom arrangement and seating patterns can be an effective means of classroom management when carefully considered and carried out. Your room arrangement should aid teaching and learning and help maintain discipline. It is important to determine what areas need to be provided and what items and types of furniture are required before you arrange the room.

The seating arrangement should focus on the chalkboard since most class instruction occurs there. You must also provide access to pencil sharpeners, reference books, learning centers, trash containers, and so on. Place these accessories, if at all possible, behind or to the side of the students' focal points, since travel to and from them can be distracting.

Seating arrangements can be used to control student behavior. Appropriate behavior may be rewarded by allowing students individually or as a group to select their own seating. Occasionally the class may even be given the opportunity to rearrange the seating as a reward for good behavior. In addition disruptive behavior may often be controlled by simply moving the disruptive student away from certain individuals or away from the total group. Placement of a disruptive student's desk beside the teacher's desk often enables the teacher to give more attention, personal contact, and encouragement to the student.

What then constitutes an effective seating arrangement? One is to seat students in shallow semicircles, no more than three rows' deep. With adequate space interspersed within the three rows, the teacher and students can travel within the arc of the semicircle with minimum disruption to working students. Moreover, this arrangement allows the teacher to move quickly to the side of a disruptive student or to provide individual assistance.

Motivation

It is impossible to deal with the causes of behavior or misbehavior without addressing the issue of motivation. Motives refer to the forces or drives that energize and direct us to act as we do. Some primary motives, such as hunger, thirst, and the need for security, are inborn. However, most of the motives you will deal with in the classroom are learned or secondary motives.

Motivation is based to a large extent on an individual's needs, attitudes, and sense of self-esteem. Figure 10.1 shows the relationship that exists among motivation, needs, attitudes, and self-esteem. The relationship is quite complex with each component causing changes in the others. As a teacher concerned with motivating students, you must be concerned with student needs, attitudes, and self-esteem.

Many scholars have proposed theories that explain why we behave as we do. The ideas of these thinkers fall into three general views: behavioral, cognitive, and humanistic. Behaviorists explain motivation in terms of external stimuli and reinforcement. The physical environment and the actions of the teacher are of prime importance to this school of thought. Cognitivists explain motivation in terms of a person's active search for meaning and satisfaction in life. Motivation is intrinsic to this group, the teacher's role being to diagnose and guide self-activated learners. Humanists stress

FIGURE 10.1   Interrelationship among Motivation, Needs, Attitudes and Self-Esteem.

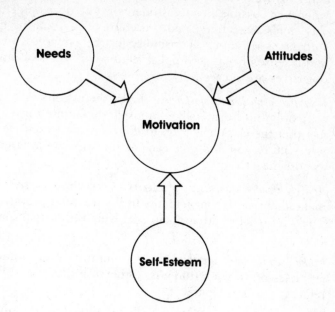

the need for personal growth and, like the cognitivists, emphasize aiding the development of intrinsic needs. Those interested in a detailed discussion of these three views of motivation should refer to any good educational psychology textbook.

How then do teachers go about motivating their students? Unfortunately there is no sure-fire method. Techniques that work in one situation or with one group of students may be totally ineffective with other situations or groups. There are, however, several general guidelines that may prove useful in motivating students..

1. *Expect the best from students.*   Research (Rosenthal and Jacobson, 1968; Brophy and Good, 1970; and Braun, 1976) reveals that students tend to live up (or down) to their teacher's expectations. Teacher expectations, then, can be used to motivate students. If you expect and demand the best from your students, you will often get it.

2. *Model desired behavior.*   Modeling is a process of teaching through example. By following your example, students will change their behavior. For example, you can model enthusiasm about what you are teaching. If your students see that you are excited about your subject, they will be, too. (And remember, enthusiasm is highly contagious. Once it infects students, the learning gains can be amazing.)

3. *Share expectations.* Share your goals and objectives with students, as well as the procedures for reaching them. In fact whenever possible involve students in the development of class goals, objectives, and procedures. This sharing gives students a sense of responsibility for their own learning and a sense of real accomplishment when the goals and objectives are successfully met.

4. *Establish a positive atmosphere.* From the beginning establish a friendly but businesslike atmosphere. Communicate the fact that the class has a job to do. Show that each student is special to you and give each as much personal attention as possible.

5. *Actively involve students.* Students are naturally active, so make them active participants in the learning process. The wise teacher attempts to use lively rather than passive activities.

6. *Make learning seem worthwhile.* Communicate the value of every lesson to your students. Otherwise they may be reluctant to participate.

7. *Cultivate self-esteem.* Everyone wants to feel important and respected. Try to plan and assign work so that every student can experience some success. Remember that repeated failure soon ends the desire to try.

8. *Capitalize on student interest.* Whenever possible relate learning to students' prior experiences and interests. Generally students pay closer attention and become more involved when the topic relates directly to their experiences and areas of interest. You should try to help students develop new interests. These can improve their attitudes toward school and even carry over into later life.

9. *Capitalize on student ideas.* Often students will willingly carry out activities that they themselves generate. Whenever possible, you should use student ideas when planning instructional activities.

10. *Capitalize on curiosity.* People are naturally curious, so add a little puzzle or suspense to your lessons. For older students the use of well-constructed questions can serve the same purpose.

11. *Challenge students.* Easy tasks soon become boring. One way to avoid boring your students is to make learning tasks challenging but not discouraging. Some students skip their school work because it is too easy; it is busy work.

This is especially true for bright students. Challenging work gives students the opportunity to test themselves and to really accomplish something. On the other hand, care should be taken that the tasks are not so difficult that they lead to frustration.

12. *Use reinforcement.* Everyone needs and wants recognition for a job well done. Carry out the principles of reinforcement as outlined in Chapter 8. Remember that rewarded behaviors are quite often repeated behaviors. All too often good behavior does not pay off, whereas misbehavior is rewarded with teacher attention and peer prestige.

13. *Use individualized instruction.* Individualized instruction is a learning plan designed specifically to meet the needs, interests, and abilities of the students involved and thus can be very motivating. Students feel in control and most often find themselves successful at the assigned tasks.

14. *Use competition.* Since students love to win and be the best, competition can often be used to motivate. But do not overuse competition. If you find that competition results in continuous failure for some students, you would be wise to turn to such alternatives as cooperative learning (where students work on tasks as a group) or even to individualized instruction.

15. *Reduce anxiety.* Students who worry and are fearful often have trouble learning. To reduce anxiety avoid putting students under unnecessary pressures. Watch your use of competition, unrealistic assignments, and exams, all of which represent areas of anxiety to students.

Motivating students is not easy. The guidelines presented here should help you begin developing your own techniques for motivating. Keep in mind that the best motivational techniques are positive in nature. Success tends to breed success.

Communications

Communication is a topic covering a broad range of complicated human relationships that are central to smoothly functioning classrooms. Since the principle ideas related to communications were addressed in detail in Chapter 6, this discussion merely summarizes the main theme of that chapter.

When problems arise in the classroom, good communications between teacher and students are essential. This means more than the "teacher talks—students listen." Real communication is an open, two-way street, in which you talk, but you also listen. As a teacher, you must learn to listen and allow students to talk and have input in finding solutions to classroom problems. You must constantly strive to improve your ability to communicate and to listen with an open mind to the feelings, ideas, and opinions of your students.

This completes our discussion of classroom atmosphere. Take a few moments to complete Task 10.2, which will check your understanding of this section.

TASK 10.2   Classroom Atmosphere

Answer the following questions. Compare your responses with those given at the end of the chapter.

1. It is usually unwise to involve students in the establishment of a positive classroom environment.   (True/False)

2. The selection and changing of student seating can be used effectively to curb disruptive behavior in the classroom.   (True/False)

3. Most of the student behaviors you encounter in the classroom are learned behaviors.   (True/False)

4. The humanistic theory of motivation is able to explain all student behavior in the classroom.   (True/False)

5. The behavioral theory of motivation places emphasis on external stimuli and the gaining of rewards for proper behaviors.   (True/False)

6. The same motivational techniques can be used effectively with all students.   (True/False)

7. Competition is always an effective motivator.   (True/False)

8. Teachers as well as students should learn to be good listeners. (True/False)

MODELS OF DISCIPLINE

Advice related to classroom management abounds. From the many models for the prevention and correction of misbehavior, we will briefly discuss six of the most popular.

The Canter Model

We will first look at **assertive discipline**. Canter and Canter (1976) advocate the need for teachers to be assertive. An assertive teacher is one who clearly and firmly communicates needs and requirements to students, follows-up with appropriate actions, responds to students in ways that maximize compliance, but in no way violates the best interests of the students (Canter and Canter, 1976, p. 9). The intent of the Canter model is to help teachers take charge in the classroom and to teach them to be calm yet forceful with students.

From the beginning of the year, assertive teachers refuse to tolerate improper behavior. Excuses such as emotional problems, poor home environment, hereditary weaknesses, and personal grievances are not accepted. The assertive teacher establishes rules for behavior along with consequences for proper and improper behavior. Students who follow the rules receive positive consequences such as some kind of material reward, free time, or special privileges, while students who break the rules receive negative consequences such as losing recess time, staying after school, or going to the principal's office. These rules and consequences are clearly communicated to students and parents at the beginning of the year.

Assertive teachers insist on decent, responsible behavior from their students. It is assumed that all students can behave if they want. Proper behavior is a matter of choice. Assertive teachers make promises, not threats, that is, they do not threaten to enforce the rules and apply the consequences; they promise to do so. Assertive teachers are consistent and follow through with action.

The Glasser Model

The Glasser model (1965) recommends reality therapy as a means to good discipline. **Reality therapy** is the act of guiding an individual toward reality; that is, assisting an individual in becoming responsible and able to satisfy his or her needs in the real world. Glasser believes that students are rational beings and can control their behavior if they wish. However, they often must be assisted in making good rather than bad choices; that is, they must be guided to become responsible individuals able to satisfy their real world needs. It is the teacher's job to provide guidance so that students make good choices. According to Glasser, this guidance is a 10-step process (Glasser, 1977).

Rules are essential to Glasser, and they must be enforced. Reasonable consequences should always follow student behavior, and no excuse should be accepted for poor behavior. Background and poor upbringing do not make poor behavior acceptable. Student responsibility must be stressed continually, and students must be forced to acknowledge their behavior and to make value judgments regarding it.

Glasser stresses the use of classroom meetings in addressing problems. Students sit in a small, close circle, discuss the problems, and seek solutions. The teacher's role is to stay in the background giving opinions only sparingly. Class rules and reasonable consequences should be developed at these meetings with all students being expected to observe them. The rules should remain flexible and open to changes at future meetings in order to accommodate changing situations.

The Kounin Model

The Kounin model (1970) stresses the ripple effect and group management. It addresses more than the prevention aspect of discipline. Kounin found that when teachers correct misbehavior in one student, it often influences behavior of nearby students. This is known as the **ripple effect**.

When misbehavior does occur in the classroom, and it will, you can prevent future occurrences of the same or similar problems by putting the ripple effect into operation. You should clearly identify the misbehaving student, what the student is doing wrong, and what the student should be doing instead. Kounin found that clarity and firmness were the important ingredients in using the ripple effect. Rough physical treatment of misbehaving students should be avoided since it tends to make the class uneasy and fearful.

Kounin also advocates the importance of teacher **withitness**, that is, the ability to know what is going on in all parts of the classroom at all times. Withit teachers are able to react quickly and accurately to class disturbances. In addition to being withit, Kounin advocates that teachers be skilled at **overlapping**, the ability to handle two or more activities or groups at the same time.

Finally Kounin notes the importance of movement management and a group focus as deterrents to behavior problems. Teachers should have the ability to make smooth lesson transitions. They should avoid "dangles" (leaving a lesson hanging while tending to something else) and "flip-flops" (changing back and forth from one subject or activity to another). They should keep students alert by holding their attention, holding them accountable for the lesson content, and involving the students in the lesson. To this end teachers should call on students randomly and occasionally call for unison responses.

The Behavior Modification Model

Behavior modification is based on the behavioral philosophy of B. F. Skinner who assumes that most behaviors are learned, that learning is largely controlled by the environment, and that behaviors that are rewarded or reinforced in some manner will occur again.

The basic premise of **behavior modification** is that behavior is changed by altering the consequences, outcomes, or rewards which follow the behavior. In this model reinforcement is used systematically to change some aspect of student behavior. Students who are good, who follow the rules, or who perform well are given reinforcers or rewards. The reinforcers may be praise, awards, grades, or even such tangible items as food or candy. Students who misbehave or who perform poorly are ignored, are removed from a reward, or are punished.

A system of reinforcement can be quite complex. One such program is the token reinforcement system. In this system, students earn tokens for both academic work and positive classroom behavior. The tokens may be points, chips, checks, play money, or anything else available. Periodically the students are given the opportunity to exchange their accumulated tokens for some desired activity or reward.

The Teacher Effectiveness Training (TET) Model

Teacher effectiveness training (TET), conceived by Dr. Thomas Gordon (1974), strives to instruct teachers in how to establish positive relationships with students. Gordon believes that teachers can reduce negative behaviors by using clearer, less provocative communications.

The TET model for dealing with classroom problems begins with the question: Who owns the problem? If the problem belongs to the student, Gordon recommends active listening (or empathetic listening) on the part of the teacher; that is, the teacher becomes a counselor and supporter. The teacher helps the student find his or her own solution to the problem. On the other hand, if the teacher owns the problem, the teacher and student must together find a solution through mutual problem solving.

The key to the use of TET is determining who owns the problem in a troublesome situation. According to Gordon, if you are blocked from reaching your goals by the student's action, then you own the problem. For example, if a student continuously makes noises as you try to teach, you own the problem because you are being kept from reaching your goal of teaching. However, if you feel annoyed by a student's behavior, if you wish a student would act differently, or if you feel embarrassed for a student, then the problem likely belongs to the student. The student who tells you that he or she hates school or hates his or her parents has the problem.

Gordon further suggests that teachers too often attack students through the use of "you" messages when, in fact, the teacher owns the problem. Rather than saying "You are slow," "You are no good," or "You are lazy," Gordon suggests that you send an I-message to tell a student how you feel about a problem situation and implicitly ask for corrective behavior. Examples of I-messages are "I am angry at what you are doing," "I am disappointed in your behavior," or "I can't hear myself think for the noise."

If an I-message does not correct the problem situation, the teacher and student are in a conflict situation. When this happens Gordon recommends that a "no-lose" problem resolution tactic be employed. The six-step no-lose tactic constitutes a form of negotiation where teacher and student contribute relatively equally. The process begins with a determination of the exact problem. Possible solutions are then generated, with the teacher and student presenting the same number of ideas. These ideas are evaluated in step three, and those unacceptable are rejected. Step four is the selection of the best solution of those that remain. This is followed by a determination of how to implement the selected solution. The last step entails an assessment of how well the solution works. Generally punishment is not recognized as a viable solution in the no-lose tactic since the student would be placed in a losing situation.

The Logical Consequences Model

The logical consequences model of discipline was originated by Rudolf Dreikurs (1982). The goal is the development of student self-discipline. Essentially the approach emphasizes that students should be taught to be responsible for their own behavior. Class rules and logical consequences for breaking the rules are developed as democratically as possible.

Logical consequences are those experiences arranged by the teacher that show students the real world. Students learn that they are responsible for their own behavior. For example if one messes the room, one cleans it. If a student fails to complete a homework assignment during class time, he or she completes it after school or at recess. Logical consequences teach students to evaluate situations, to learn from experiences, and to make responsible choices.

Dreikurs further suggests that students want to belong and gain acceptance and that their behavior is directed toward achieving this goal. Thus students misbehave because they are under the mistaken belief that it will get them the acceptance they desire. Dreikurs calls these beliefs mistaken goals. The four mistaken goals are: attention getting, power seeking, revenge seeking, and desire to be left alone.

The key to correcting a behavior problem lies in identifying the mistaken goal and making the student understand that it is prompting the problem behavior. The student is informed of the logical consequences of the behavior and commits to good behavior.

The six models of discipline that have been discussed in this section can be characterized by certain similarities and differences. Table 10.2 summarizes the general characteristics of the six models, the X's indicating which model puts special emphasis on the stated characteristics. However, keep in mind that the other models might also address the characteristic to a limited degree. Study Table 10.2 and complete Task 10.3, which checks your understanding of the six models.

TABLE 10.2 Characteristics of Discipline Models.

	CANTER MODEL	GLASSER MODEL	KOUNIN MODEL	BEHAVIOR MOD	TET	LOGICAL CONSE-QUENCES
Encourages responsible behavior		x				x
Rules established	x	x		x		x
Consequences for inappropriate behavior	x			x		x
Use of ripple effect			x			
Reinforcement of appropriate behavior	x			x		
Negotiated conflict resolution					x	
Effort to make student aware of origins of their behavior		x			x	x
Setting of clear limits	x	x		x		x
Goal of self-discipline		x			x	x
Behavior is goal directed				x		x
Emphasis on prevention			x			
Emphasis on communications					x	

SOURCE: Adapted from Duke and Meckel (1984), *Teacher's Guide to Classroom Management*. New York: Random House. Used with permission.

TASK 10.3 The Models of Discipline

We have briefly discussed six models of discipline. Each of the following statements represents a position from one of the models. Identify each position as representative of the Canter model (CT), the Glasser model (GL), the Kounin model (KO), the behavior modification model (BM), the teacher effectiveness training model (TET), or the logical consequences model (LC). Compare your responses with those given at the end of the chapter.

_____ 1. The teacher reduces the occurrences of inappropriate behavior by establishing a positive, helping relationship with students.

_____ 2. The teacher rewards acceptable student behavior and ignores unacceptable student behavior.

_____ 3. The teacher takes charge in the classroom and is assertive and firm.

_____ 4. The teacher identifies and makes students aware of their mistaken goals when they misbehave.

_____ 5. The teacher uses the ripple effect when a student misbehaves.

_____ 6. The teacher establishes rules and continuously stresses student responsibility.

_____ 7. The teacher uses classroom meetings to discuss and handle problem situations.

_____ 8. The teacher allows students to suffer the natural consequences when they misbehave, thus showing them the real world.

_____ 9. The teacher communicates an awareness of knowing what is going on in the classroom at all times.

_____ 10. The teacher views a token reinforcement system as an effective means of promoting proper student behavior.

_____ 11. The teacher uses I-messages rather than you-messages when problem situations occur.

_____ 12. The teacher communicates needs and requirements to students and follows-up words with actions.

_____ 13. The teacher assists students in making good choices rather than bad choices.

_____ 14. The teacher uses the no-lose tactic when confronted with a conflict situation.

Every classroom teacher must eventually develop his or her own approach to classroom management. On the basis of the preceding discussion, which approach or approaches embody concepts that you feel fit your own educational philosophy? Perhaps some combination of approaches will be suitable for you. These are decisions you must make in implementing a management system in your own classroom.

CONTROL TECHNIQUES

Only you can develop an overall approach to discipline that is appropriate for your classroom. However, based on the discussion of classroom management to this point, several control techniques appear to be characteristic of effective classroom managers. We now look at some of these techniques.

Setting Limits

Students need and want limits (rules). They want to know what is expected of them and why. Teachers who try to avoid setting limits and imposing necessary structure will often find that chaos results, particularly when dealing with younger children.

Clarity and consistency are vital in the establishment of rules. You should explain why certain rules are needed or even better involve students in a discussion as to why certain rules are necessary. Your rules should always reinforce the basic idea that students are in school to study and learn. Moreover avoid too many rules, unnecessary rules, and above all, unenforceable rules. When no longer needed, a rule should be discarded or changed. However, so long as they are retained, rules must be enforced.

It is often better to have a few general rules (five or six) that cover many specifics rather than trying to list all the specifics. But if specific actions represent a problem area, then a rule should cover the specific problem. Examples of appropriate general classroom rules are:

1. Be polite and respectful
2. Take care of your classroom
3. Do not hit, shove, or hurt others
4. Follow directions
5. Obtain permission before speaking or leaving your seat
6. Be prepared with books, paper, pencil, and so on when you come to class

Your rules should always be discussed with students. Specific behaviors that are included and excluded in each general rule should be explained and discussed. With younger children you should post the rules, whereas with older students it is wise to have them record the rules for future reference. You should also consider sending parents a copy of your classroom rules.

As soon as you decide on your rules, you must consider what to do when a student breaks a rule. It is too late to make this decision after the rule has been broken. For many classroom infractions, a logical consequence is to have the students correct their mistakes. Incomplete papers can be finished or redone; messes can be cleaned up. For other infractions you may want to form a graduated series of consequences, such as:

First infraction: Name on board

Second infraction: Lose lunch recess

Third infraction: Teacher conference

Fourth infraction: Conference with principal

Fifth infraction: Parent conference

When infractions occur, avoid, if at all possible, a direct classroom confrontation. Instead ask the student to refrain from the behavior. If the student responds negatively and continues the behavior, ask the student to leave the room and wait outside until you are free to have a private conference. At this conference address the undesired behavior, the consequences of that behavior, and the student's responsibility as a member of the class. If the behavior continues after the conference, you should seek the principal's assistance.

If you have determined the rules for your classroom and the consequences for breaking the rules, you have made the first step in having a well-managed classroom. You must now get the year started right.

Getting Started

The first few weeks of the school year are of prime importance with regard to management. They set the stage for the year and establish your credibility. In fact, it can be predicted from what you do during the first few weeks both how well you will manage your classroom and the extent of student engagement in learning tasks.

What do effective managers do during those first critical weeks? Based upon our discussion to this point and related research, to be an effective manager you should develop and establish an efficient organizational system and supporting classroom procedures. For example you must arrange student seating and storage of materials, establish procedures for starting and ending class, establish lesson procedures, and set up homework procedures and policies. The classroom focus during the first few weeks of school should be teaching your system and procedures. You should establish a positive classroom environment, establish rules and consequences, and above all plan well and make your content meaningful to the students. It is also important to communicate your expectations to your students and to establish an atmosphere of free exchange. Invite students' cooperation. Develop self-discipline by having students analyze their own behavior. Finally be firm, organized, and consistent in your expectations of students.

What about the problem of the teacher who enters a class after the beginning of the term and does not have access to early focus on an organizational system and supporting classroom procedures? Again, the first task is to establish credibility. Communicate your expectations to students, discuss changes in classroom procedures that are needed to support the expectations, and, above all, be firm and consistent with regard to the expectations.

Likewise, what about new students who enter a class during the term? Here again, the student must be made aware of your expectations, organizational system, and classroom procedures. This task can often be accomplished in a private conference with appropriate reminders given as needed in class.

Ripple Effect

Any time a student is corrected or punished for misbehaving, the impact is felt not only by the student but also by other students in the class. Although this ripple effect can help establish the ground rules of your classroom, it can also be harmful to the overall classroom atmosphere.

When a student tests your enforcement of the rules, and one always will, you cannot ignore it. If you do, the fact that the student got away with something "ripples out" to other students and encourages them to test you. Conversely when you stand firm and consistently apply your rules and consequences, this action too will ripple out to other students. They will be less likely to try you in the future.

Care must be taken in correcting students. Some students become nervous and fearful when someone is treated harshly. They may lose their desire to learn. Therefore, use care in correcting student behavior in front of the class. Correct misbehavior in an unobtrusive manner if at all possible, using the least force necessary for getting the job done. In addition address the problem behavior itself rather than ridiculing or putting the student down as a person. Be direct, fair, open, and respectful with students when correcting their behavior.

Criticism

Avoid criticism; it just provokes hostility. The student may blow up and say something unintentional or may even give up trying. To "put down" a student in front of his or her peers is probably one of the most damaging things you can do to a student.

Students react more favorably if your criticism is in the form of a suggestion. Better yet, take the student aside, out of earshot of others, and deal with the problem in a matter-of-fact manner.

Rewards

All behavior must have some kind of pay off (reward, reinforcer, etc.), which can be anything that causes a behavior to increase. With some students the pay off is intrinsic, the inner satisfaction of doing well or doing the right thing. However, some students need extrinsic rewards for behaving properly. You would be wise to include a reward of some type for following the established rules. This reward could include such things as stickers, free time, a popcorn party, toys, or anything desirable to your students.

Some people feel that granting rewards is tantamount to bribing students. However, the dictionary defines bribing as "receiving money or favors for doing something illegal or immoral." Helping a student to learn or to achieve self control does not fit this definition.

This concludes our discussion of the various control techniques that can be used in the classroom. Let us finish our discussion of classroom management by looking at some general guidelines related to effective management.

MANAGEMENT GUIDELINES

Managing a classroom is a difficult but essential task if you are going to teach. The discussion thus far has been based on the theory and research of classroom management scholars. Sometimes, however, experience is the best teacher for learning to manage a classroom. The following are teacher-tested suggestions for managing a classroom and preventing behavior problems.

1. *Begin class on time.*   When the bell rings, require that everyone be in their seat. Require that all talking stop.

2. *Set up procedures for beginning your class.*   You should have a set routine or activity that automatically occupies the first four or five minutes of class.

3. *Set up procedures for dismissing class.*   Require that all students be in their seats and quiet before they are dismissed. This prevents most problems that develop as students rush to leave.

4. *Keep desks and storage areas clean.*   Set aside a particular period of time to clean out desks and storage areas.

5. *Stop misbehavior immediately.*   Send nonverbal cues (making eye contact, moving in that direction, pointing toward his or her work) to the offender. Tell the student the correct procedure or rule in a clear, assertive, and unhostile manner.

6. *Make transitions between activities quick and orderly.*   Give all directions before any movement begins or before materials are passed out. Students should know where they are expected to go and what they are expected to do when they get there.

7. *Direct your talk to the class not to the chalkboard.*   Make eye contact with your students as you talk. It is usually unwise to turn your back to the class for long periods.

8. *Be polite to students and reinforce their politeness.*   Communicate to the class that you expect their cooperation. Never use sarcasm in communicating your desires to students.

9. *Be firm and consistent.*   If a rule is broken, warn students only once, then follow through with the consequences. Do not let yourself be talked out of a position you have taken or the consequences to breaking a rule.

10. *Do not threaten.*   Do not take a position or make a threat that you cannot hold or carry out. Do not make threats; make promises.

11. *Be withit.*   Move around the room and know what is going on in all areas. Do not become engrossed with a few students and forget that you are in charge of a class.

12. *Use nonverbal signals.*   The use of nonverbal signals and body language is one of the best ways to prevent discipline problems. Examples are a frown, a nod, movement toward the student, an intent look, and a raised hand.

13. *Be helpful, not hurtful.*   Show students you want to support their best behaviors and help them develop their own self-discipline.

14. *Use corporal punishment only as a last resort.*   Try other approaches first, as corporal punishment generally does not work well.

15. *Plan well.*   You should enter your classroom every day with well-planned lessons that involve all students in activities that have specific, clear-cut goals.

16. *Use verbal reprimands with care.*   Avoid nagging and the use of sarcasm, ridicule, and loud, frequent reprimands. They are ineffective. Instead use calm, firm reprimands and, as a rule, deliver your reprimands in private.

7. *Always set a good example.*   Remember, you are a model for classroom behavior. Do as you would be done to. Do not take yourself too seriously. Develop a sense of humor.

This concludes our discussion of various discipline guidelines. If you can successfully carry out these guidelines, it will prevent most of the problems you will encounter in your classroom. Take a few moments to complete Task 10.4, which will check your understanding of the material presented in the last two sections.

TASK 10.4 Management Techniques and Guidelines

Answer the following questions. Compare your responses with those given at the end of the chapter.

1. Rules should always be stated specifically; never state a rule in general terms.   (True/False)

2. It is usually good policy to start the school year off by being rather firm.   (True/False)

3. The ripple effect can be used effectively to curb misbehavior in the classroom.   (True/False)

4. The use of sarcasm, criticism, ridicule, harsh or humiliating punishments can be effective as management techniques.   (True/False)

5. One should avoid giving students a reward for desired behavior since it amounts to bribery.   (True/False)

6. Nonverbal communications is an important component of classroom management.   (True/False)

7. Corporal punishment is one of the most effective management techniques that a teacher can use in managing a classroom. (True/False)

8. It is usually good policy to give reprimands in front of the whole class. (True/False)

SUMMARY

The importance of classroom management can hardly be exaggerated. A classroom must have an effective leader, be orderly, and discipline must be maintained for learning to take place. Thus, good classroom management on your part is essential if you are to be a successful teacher.

The key to effective management is the relationship you establish with your students. Promote a democratic (sharing of responsibility) but businesslike atmosphere in your classroom. However, remember that you are the classroom authority and should always act as such. Avoid authoritarian (compliance through force) and laissez-faire (anything goes) techniques. Students need to know where they stand and where they are going.

The start of the school year often sets the general atmosphere of the classroom. Start your year with a bang. Plan your classes well. Establish your rules, with student input if possible. Plan consequences for breaking the rules. Be sure everyone understands the need and the reasons for the rules and consequences. Be consistent and fair in the enforcement of rules. Finally be firm in the beginning; you can be less strict later on.

As a final thought, keep in mind that students want structure and need limits. It is your responsibility to provide leadership, to provide classroom structure, and to set classroom limits. The atmosphere you establish in your classroom should give students the opportunity to work on and to develop a sense of self-discipline.

Answer Keys

TASK 10.1   Identifying Leadership Styles

1. D   2. A   3. A   4. D   5. D   6. L

TASK 10.2   Classroom Atmosphere

1. *False*   Students can and should be involved in establishing a positive classroom environment. It then becomes their room.

2. *True*   The selection and changing of seating is an important aspect of classroom management. Desks that are too close to each other or in the traffic patterns often represent distractions to working students.

3. *True*   Students have learned to behave in certain ways to obtain desired rewards.

4. *False*   All three theories of motivation (behavioral, cognitive, and humanistic) are needed to explain the behavior of students.

5. *True*   This school of thought believes that we only do things for some type of external reward.

6. *False*   Successful motivational techniques vary with different students and different situations.

7. *False*   Competition may have a negative effect if some students lose all the time.

8. *True*   Teachers tend to talk too much and fail to listen enough.

TASK 10.3   The Models of Discipline

The following responses would be appropriate. However, some of your responses might be different. Some of the statements might represent more than one model depending on our interpretation. Therefore, when you disagree with this key, analyze your response carefully. If you feel comfortable with the response, stand by it.

1. TET	2. BM	3. CT	4. LC	5. KO
6. GL	7. GL	8. LC	9. KO	10. BM
11. TET	12. CT	13. GL	14. TET	

TASK 10.4   Management Techniques and Guidelines

1. *False* It is often best to have a few general rules. The specifics of these general rules should be discussed with students.

2. *True* A firm, businesslike start communicates to students that they are in class to learn.

3. *True* The impact of correcting misbehavior in one student is often felt by other students in the class.

4. *False* Sarcasm, criticism, ridicule, and harsh or humiliating punishment should be avoided. These techniques often provoke hostility and a desire for revenge on the part of students.

5. *False* It is not bribery to help someone improve on achievement or self-control.

6. *True* A strong nonverbal cue in an offender's direction is often all that is needed to stop misbehavior.

7. *False* Use corporal punishment only as a last resort.

8. *False* When given in front of the class, a student often feels a need to respond negatively to save face with the peer group.

ACTIVITIES

1. *Causes of misbehavior* Think back over the classes you have observed and attended in which there have been disciplinary incidents. List all the possible causes for the student misbehaviors. How might knowledge of the causes of these misbehaviors influence a teacher's action? Some behavior problems are teacher created. Can you think of some examples?

2. *Behavior observation* Complete several observations in various classrooms at different levels. How do the observed teachers control behavior? Do the teachers use signals, warnings, nonverbal messages, or other subtle measures to prevent disci-

pline problems from arising? Which techniques seem most successful? Do all students respond the same way? Does there appear to be a difference in effectiveness at the various grade levels?

3. *Model analysis* Analyze the six models of discipline. Which model, if any, do you prefer? Can you put together parts of the different models and come up with a plan you think would work for you? Can you identify some basic concepts that appear to be true of all six models?

4. *Planning* Plan a first day for a class you may teach. What introductory activities would you use? What rules and consequences would you introduce and discuss? What would you do to motivate your students?

REFERENCES

————. (1981), *Crossroads . . . A Handbook for Effective Classroom Management.* Oklahoma State Department of Education.

Bethel, L. J., and George, K. D. (February 1979). Classroom control. *Science and Children,* 24–5.

Brawn, C. (Spring 1976). Teacher expectation: Sociopsychological dynamics. *Review of Educational Research,* 46(2), 185–212.

Brophy, J. E., and Good, T. L. (1970). Teacher's communication of differential expectations for children's classroom performance: Some behavioral data. *Journal of Educational Psychology,* 61, 365–74.

Canter, L., and Canter, M. (1976). *Assertive Discipline: A Take-Charge Approach for Today's Educator.* Los Angeles: Canter and Associates.

Charles, C. M. (1981). *Building Classroom Discipline.* New York: Longman.

Drew, W. F., Olds, A. R., and Olds, H. F., Jr. (1974). *Motivating Today's Students.* Palo Alto, Calif.: Learning Handbooks.

Dreikurs, R., and Cassel, P. (1974). *Discipline Without Tears,* 2d ed. New York: Hawthorn Books.

Dreikurs, R., Grunwald, B. B., and Pepper, F. C. (1982). *Maintaining Sanity in the Classroom,* 2d ed. New York: Harper and Row.

Duke, D. L., and Meckel, A. M. (1984). *Teacher's Guide to Classroom Management.* New York: Random House.

Appendix A _____

Microteaching

Microteaching is a scaled down teaching situation in which a 5- or 10-minute mini-lesson demonstrating one or more specific skills is taught to a few students. It is often an integral component of methods classes in a preparatory program where the various skills and behaviors addressed are practiced and demonstrated. Microteaching can also be used effectively by in-service teachers to practice new instructional skills or behaviors. Each session focuses on a specific aspect of teaching until a satisfactory level of mastery is demonstrated. Lessons are usually videotaped, played back, and critiqued by the teacher trainee and the instructor.

Microteaching simplifies the task of teaching by reducing the length and complexity of a lesson. Teaching a shorter, more specific lesson enables a teacher trainee to focus on a few major skills in the planning process. In addition, it provides an opportunity for constructive feedback from both the students being taught and an instructor. Videotaping a microteaching lesson offers a further advantage because the tape can be replayed as many times as necessary. The instructor and students can focus on different aspects of the lesson with each viewing.

Before teaching a microteaching lesson, however, the experience must be carefully planned. First, the teacher trainee must select the skills or behaviors that will be practiced in the short time span. For example, he or she may want to demonstrate effective questioning techniques; appropriate use of reinforcement; effective use of stimulus variation; use of a specific teaching method (discussion, lecture, inquiry, exposition with interaction, etc.); or some combination of these skills or behaviors.

Second, the teacher trainee must select a topic that will be appropriate for demonstrating the selected skills or behaviors. Due to time constraints, this topic must be somewhat narrow—a single subconcept that can be taught in a 5- to 10-minute time span.

Third, as in regular daily planning, the teacher trainee should carefully specify the objectives. In fact, it is often wise to limit teaching to one objective in a microteaching lesson. The preparation form that follows can be used as a guide to aid in planning for a microteaching lesson. After completing this form, the teacher trainee should prepare a lesson plan using a form similar to the Microteaching Preparation Form.

Finally, a set of criteria must be established by which to judge mastery of the desired skill(s) or behavior(s). It is often helpful to develop and use an evaluation form or a recording instrument that reflects the stated criteria. A form such as the following Microteaching Evaluation Form or Microteaching Self-Analysis Form may be of some assistance in the design of similar evaluative instruments. Such forms should be completed by the students taught, the instructor, and the teacher trainee as a tape of the microteaching session is replayed for analysis. The feedback obtained from the completed forms should be analyzed by the teacher trainee with respect to mastery of stated skills or behaviors. This analysis will help to identify specific teaching skills that need improvement as well as to develop the skills needed to study teaching behavior for purposes of self-improvement. These self-improvement skills will be invaluable when the teacher trainee becomes a classroom teacher.

MICROTEACHING PREPARATION FORM

Use this form for initial preparation of your lesson. After completing this form prepare a formal lesson plan.

1. Skill(s) or behavior(s) to demonstrate: _____

   _____

   _____

   _____

2. Subconcept to teach: _____

   _____

   _____

   _____

3. Specific instructional objective(s): _____

   _____

   _____

   _____

4. Strategies to use: _____

   _____

   _____

   _____

5. Student experiences to provide: _____

   _____

   _____

   _____

6. Materials and equipment needed: _____

   _____

   _____

   _____

LESSON PLAN FORMAT

Teacher: _____ Date: _____

Course Title: _____ Grade Level: _____

Subconcept: _____

_____

Instructional objective(s): _____

_____

_____

Rationale: _____

_____

Introduction: _____

_____

_____

CONTENT	INSTRUCTIONAL PROCEDURES
	(a)
	(b)
	(c)
	(d)
	(e)

Closure: _____

_____

_____

Evaluation procedure: _____

_____

_____

Materials and aids: _____

_____

_____

MICROTEACHING EVALUATION FORM

Teacher: _____ Date: _____

Subject: _____

Rate the teacher trainee on each skill area. Code: 5 or 4, mastery of skill demonstrated; 3 or 2, some skill refinement needed; and 1 or 0, much skill refinement needed.

Organization of Lesson

5 4 3 2 1 0   Lesson preparation

5 4 3 2 1 0   Lesson introduction

5 4 3 2 1 0   Subject-matter knowledge

5 4 3 2 1 0   Closure

Comments: _____

_____

_____

_____

Lesson Presentation

5 4 3 2 1 0   Audience contact

5 4 3 2 1 0   Enthusiasm

5 4 3 2 1 0   Speech quality and delivery

5 4 3 2 1 0   Involvement of audience

5 4 3 2 1 0   Use of nonverbal communications

5 4 3 2 1 0   Use of questions

5 4 3 2 1 0   Directions and refocusing

5 4 3 2 1 0   Use of reinforcement

5 4 3 2 1 0   Use of aids and materials

Comments: _____

_____

_____

_____

224

MICROTEACHING SELF-ANALYSIS FORM

Teacher: _____ Date: _____

Subconcept taught: _____

Replay the tape of your microteaching session as needed to collect data for the following items. Analyze the collected data and draw conclusions with respect to the behavior addressed in each item.

1. Teacher talk versus student talk.   Set up a small chart as follows:

   Teacher talk: _____

   Student talk: _____

   Silence or confusion: _____

   As you view your microteaching tape, place a tally on the chart to represent who was talking approximately every three seconds. If no one was talking or if many people were talking simultaneously, then place a tally in the silence or confusion category. When you have finished, count the number of tallies in each category as well as the total number of tallies in the categories teacher talk and student talk combined. Use the following formulas to determine the percentage of teacher talk and student talk:

   $$\% \begin{array}{c} \text{Teacher} \\ \text{Talk} \end{array} = \frac{\text{Tallies in teacher talk category}}{\text{Tallies in teacher talk } + \text{ student talk categories}} \times 100$$

   $$\% \begin{array}{c} \text{Student} \\ \text{Talk} \end{array} = \frac{\text{Tallies in student talk category}}{\text{Tallies in teacher talk } + \text{ student talk categories}} \times 100$$

2. Filler words.   Record the filler words or sounds ("okay," "you know," or "uh") and the number of times each was used: _____

   _____

   _____

   _____

   _____

3. Questions.   Record the number of questions asked:

   Convergent: _____

   Divergent: _____

4. Student names.   Record the number of times students are addressed by name:

   _____

(continued)

5. Pauses.   Record the number of times pauses are used to give students time to think: _____

6. Reinforcement.   Record the number of times reinforcement is used.

   Verbal reinforcement: _____

   Nonverbal reinforcement: _____

7. Sensory channels.   Record the number of times students are required to change sensory channel: _____

Glossary

Achievement test   Standardized test designed to measure knowledge of a particular subject or battery of subjects.

Advance organizer   An introductory statement to students that provides a structure for new information that is to be presented.

Analysis   Cognitive learning that entails breaking down material into its constituent parts so it can be understood.

Application   Cognitive learning that entails the use of rules or processes in new and concrete situations.

Assertive discipline   A classroom management approach developed by Canter and Canter that stresses the need for teachers to communicate in clear, firm, unhostile terms classroom needs and requirements.

Behavior   Actions that are observable and overt; they must be seen and should be countable.

Behavior modification   The manipulation of observable behavior by altering the consequences, outcomes, or rewards that follow the behavior.

Check list   A list of criteria, or things to look for, which some performance or end product is to be judged.

Closure   See **lesson closure**.

Cognitive set   See **set induction**.

Commitment   Affective learning that involves building an internally consistent value system and freely living by it.

Comprehension   Cognitive learning that entails changing the form of previously learned material or making simple interpretations.

Continuous reinforcement schedule   A pattern in which every occurrence of a desired action is reinforced.

Convergent questions   Questions that have only one correct response.

Creation   Cognitive learning that entails combining elements and parts in order to form a new whole or to produce an evaluation based on specified criteria.

Delayed reinforcement   Reinforcement of a desired action that took place at an earlier time.

Descriptive data   Data that have been organized, categorized, or quantified by an observer but do not involve a value judgment.

Divergent questions   Questions for which there are many correct responses.

Duration measurement   The length of time an observable behavior continues or the time interval between the communication of a direction or signal and the occurrence of the required observable behavior.

Empirical questions   Questions that require integration or analysis of remembered or given information in order to supply a predictable answer.

Evaluation   The process of obtaining available information about students and using it to ascertain the degree of change in the students' performance.

Evaluative questions   Questions that require that a judgment be made or a value be put on something.

Extinction   The gradual disappearance of a behavior through the removal or withholding of reinforcement.

Extrinsic motivation   Motivation created by events or rewards outside the individual.

Factual questions   Questions that require the recall of information through the mental processes of recognition and rote memory.

Fixed reinforcement schedule   A pattern in which reinforcement is dispensed after a desired observable behavior has occurred a constant number of times or has occurred for a constant length of time.

Focusing questions   Questions used to focus students' attention on a lesson or on the content of a lesson.

Formative evaluation   Evaluation that takes place both before and during the learning process and is used to promote learning.

Frequency measurement   A measure of the number of times specified observable behaviors are exhibited in a constant time interval.

Goals Extremely broad statements of school or instructional purposes.

Halting time A teacher pause in talking used to give students time to think about presented materials or directions.

Imitation Psychomotor ability to carry out the basic rudiments of a skill when given directions and supervision.

Inference The process of interpreting direct observations to form interpretive conclusions.

Informational objectives Statements of learning intent that are abbreviations of instructional objectives in that only the student performance and the product are specified.

Instructional objectives A clear and unambiguous description of instructional intent with student performance, product, conditions, and criterion specified.

Intermittent reinforcement schedule A pattern in which correct responses are reinforced often but not following each occurrence of the desirable behavior.

Interval reinforcement schedule A pattern in which reinforcement is dispensed after desired observable behavior has occurred for a specified length of time.

Intrinsic motivation An internal source of motivation associated with activities that are rewarding in themselves.

Knowledge learning Cognitive learning that entails the simple recall of learned materials.

Learning A relatively permanent change in an individual's capacity for performance as a result of experience.

Lesson closure Teacher actions and statements designed to make a lesson content understandable and meaningful and to bring the presentation to an appropriate conclusion.

Likert scale A five-point attitude scale with linked options strongly agree, agree, undecided, disagree, and strongly disagree.

Manipulation Psychomotor ability to perform a skill independently.

Measurement The assignment of numerical values to objects, events, performances, or products to indicate the degree to which they possess the characteristic being measured.

Negative reinforcement Strengthening the likelihood of a behavior or event by the removal of an unpleasant stimulus.

Nonverbal reinforcement Using some form of physical action as a positive consequence to strengthen a behavior or event.

Objective A clear and unambiguous description of instructional intent.

Overlapping A teacher's ability to attend to and supervise several activities simultaneously.

Planning A sequential decision-making process where it is decided what should be taught, how best to teach the desired content or skills, and how to best determine whether the content or skills have been mastered.

Positive reinforcement Strengthening the likelihood of a behavior or event by the presentation of a desired stimulus.

Precision Psychomotor ability to perform an act accurately, efficiently, and harmoniously.

Premack principle The use of a preferred activity as reinforcement for a less-preferred activity.

Probing questions Questions that follow a student response and require the student to think and respond more thoroughly than the initial response.

Productive questions Broad open-ended questions with many correct responses that require students to use their imagination, to think creatively, and to produce something unique.

Prompting questions Questions that involve the use of hints and clues to aid students in answering questions or to assist students in correcting an initial response.

Qualified reinforcement Reinforcement of only the acceptable parts of an individual's response or action or of the attempt itself.

Questionnaire A list of written statements regarding attitudes, feelings, and opinions that are read and responded to.

Rating scale A scale of values arranged in order of quality describing someone or something being evaluated.

Ratio reinforcement schedule Pattern in which reinforcement is dispensed after a desired observable behavior has occurred a certain number of times.

Reality therapy   The act of assisting individuals in becoming responsible individuals able to satisfy their needs in the real world.

Receiving   Affective learning that involves being aware of and willing to freely attend to a stimulus.

Redirecting   The techniques of asking several individuals to respond to a question in light of or to add new insight to the previous responses.

Reflective listening   The act of listening with feeling as well as with cognition.

Reinforcement   Using consequences to strengthen the likelihood of a behavior or event.

Reliability   The consistency of test scores obtained in repeated administrations to the same individuals on different occasions or with different sets of equivalent items.

Reproduced data   Data that have been recorded in video, audio, or verbatim transcript form and can be reproduced when desired.

Responding   Affective learning that involves freely attending to a stimulus as well as voluntarily reacting to it in some way.

Ripple effect   The spreading of behaviors from one individual to others through imitation.

Semantic differential   A seven-point scale that links an adjective to its opposite; designed so that attitudes, feelings, and opinions can be measured by degree, from very favorable to highly unfavorable.

Set induction   Teacher actions and statements at the outset of a lesson to get student attention, to trigger interest, and to establish a conceptual framework.

Silent time   The time the teacher waits following a student response before replying or continuing with the presentation.

Standardized test   A commercially developed test that samples behavior under uniform procedures.

Summative evaluation   Evaluation used to determine the extent of student learning on completion of instruction.

Teacher-made test   An evaluative instrument developed and scored by a teacher to meet particular classroom needs.

Teaching   The actions of someone trying to assist others to reach their fullest potential in all aspects of development.

Time-sample measurement   A sampling of the environment for specific observable behaviors at predetermined time intervals.

Token reinforcement system   By performing teacher-desired actions or behaviors, students earn neutral tokens that can be exchanged periodically for rewards.

Usability   The practical considerations such as cost, time to administer, difficulty, and scoring procedure of a test.

Validity   The ability of a test to measure what it purports to.

Valued data   Data that involve a value judgment on the part of an observer.

Valuing   Affective learning that involves voluntarily giving worth to an object, a phenomenon, or a stimulus.

Variable reinforcement schedule   A pattern in which the number of desired responses or the length of time desired responses have occurred varies between the dispensing of reinforcement.

Verbal component   The actual words and the meaning of a spoken message.

Verbal reinforcement   Using positive comments as consequences to strengthen a behavior or event.

Vicarious reinforcement   An individual's strengthening of a behavior or an event in order to receive the consequences obtained by others who exhibit the same behavior.

Vocal component   The meaning attached to a spoken message resulting from such variables as voice firmness, modulation, tone, tempo, pitch, and loudness.

Wait time 1   The initial time a teacher waits following a question before calling for the response.

Wait time 2   The total time a teacher waits for all students to respond to the same question or for students to respond to each others' responses to a question.

Withitness   A teacher's awareness of what is going on in all parts of the classroom and the ability to communicate this awareness.

Index

DATE DUE			

HIGHSMITH 45-220